Weaving Designs for Needlepoint

Weaving Designs for Needlepoint

BY SALLY NICOLETTI

Photographs by John McKee,

William Froelich and Joseph Nicoletti

Graphs by D. Andrew Eddy and Sally Nicoletti

Diagrams by Mary Hoffman Treworgy

William Morrow and Company, Inc.   New York

Book design by Sallie Baldwin, ANTLER & BALDWIN, INC.

Library of Congress Cataloging in Publication Data
Nicoletti, Sally.
 Weaving designs for needlepoint.

 Bibliography: p.
 1. Canvas embroidery—Patterns. 2. Weaving—
Patterns. I. Title.
TT778.C3N52   746.4'4   78-5878
ISBN 0-688-03330-X

PRINTED IN THE UNITED STATES OF AMERICA.
First Edition
1 2 3 4 5 6 7 8 9 10

To Joe

Acknowledgments

I wish to express my deepest gratitude to the many, many people without whose generous help and support this book would not have been possible:

to my husband, Joseph Nicoletti, for his unfailing support and help,

to Pamela Hatch, for her enthusiastic support and editorial guidance in the early stages,

to Narcisse Chamberlain, for graciously carrying on,

to Pat Robinson, for her continued encouragement and generosity,

to Eve Rittmeyer and Elena Silander, who helped keep me organized,

to Sally Bond at the Peabody Museum and Barbara Teague at the Metropolitan Museum, who helped me with my research,

to Amy Smith, at whose suggestion I first began to consider putting this book together,

to Bucilla, who most graciously consented to supply the beautiful yarns with which the designs were worked,

and to all of the kind, skillful people who stitched the designs, proofed the graphs, and did the finishing work, listed on pages 179–180.

Contents

List of Illustrations

Weaving Designs for Needlepoint

Introduction

At some point in my work as a designer of needlepoint canvases, I began to be aware of a strong attraction to handwoven textiles of various cultures as sources of design. Much of the appeal of a remarkable piece of weaving lies in the sense of human presence with which it is graced. It seems to reflect the intelligence, intuition, and industry by which it came into being and to embody the character of the time and place in which it was woven.

The elements of timelessness and universality, inherent in everything that people consider beautiful, speak to us over time and distance and distinguish the particular work from other products of craft and function. So the enduring nature of a beautiful woven design seems appropriate to the effort and time one invests in a work of needlepoint, particularly considering the long-wearing, durable quality of the resulting needlepoint fabric.

The process of weaving, by its very nature, tends to produce designs compatible with the character of needlepoint. Natural forms and phenomena are abstracted to simple, evocative shapes and colors, each serving a symbolic function in an often complex total image. These shapes from the warp and weft of the loom seem more at home with the horizontal and vertical threads of the needlepoint canvas than do the more naturalistic or "painterly" representations of flora and fauna typical of traditional needlepoint.

With all of this in mind, I have assembled a collection of designs to be worked in needlepoint that are derived from the woven images of many cultures, most of which are rarely seen outside of museums. In adapting these from the medium of weaving to the medium of needlepoint, I have found that the latter imposes certain limitations of its own. I have therefore tried to respect these limitations and, at the same time, to preserve the complexity and integrity of the original woven design.

I do hope you will enjoy working these designs and living with them for a long time to come.

The Basics

Materials

There are many types of needlepoint canvases, yarns, and needles, but the designs in this book require only the most basic discussion of a few of them:

CANVAS

This is available in a number of gauges (threads per inch) and in several types of manufacture. The two types I recommend for adapting woven designs are:

Interlocked mono canvas—composed of intertwined double threads running horizontally and vertically, locking where they mesh.

Plain mono canvas—single threads (usually cotton), running horizontally and vertically, not interlocked.

Preparing the Canvas:

The directions for each design specify how large a piece of canvas you will need, providing for an inch of unworked margin from the edge of the design to the raw edge of the canvas all around; therefore, the dimensions given for canvas include at least an extra two inches horizontally and vertically.

You may secure the raw edges of the canvas by applying masking tape (3/4" wide is sufficient). Or, you may stitch double-fold bias tape around the edges with a sewing machine; trim corners in order to ease the bias tape around. Always mark "top" along the upper taped edge in order to maintain your orientation when you put down the canvas and pick it up again.

For a number of exactly square designs in this book, you may wish to use canvas which, when the mesh are counted each way, will measure to be an almost perfect square. Most canvas available will yield a slightly longer edge one way. Perfectly square canvas is referred to as "deluxe quality Zweigart" canvas or "orange-lined" canvas. If this is not obtainable in your area, write Joan Toggitt, Ltd. (see SOURCES).

YARNS

Persian Yarn:

This high-quality wool yarn, made especially for embroidery, is available in a wide range of colors. It is always characterized by being composed of three separate threads plied together. It is best to work with lengths of about 18 inches to 22 inches to avoid knotting and fraying of the yarn. However, when using a full strand on 10-mesh-to-the-inch canvas, longer lengths are usually fine to work with—whatever you find most comfortable.

To achieve fuller, "healthier-looking" stitches, separate the yarn into its three separate threads, or two threads, whichever you are working with, and hold them together while stitching. This is especially important to do when you are working a Bargello type of stitch, such as the straight Gobelin, in order to avoid having too much of the canvas peeking through.

You "anchor" the first end of the yarn by holding an inch or so of it at the back of the canvas while working your stitches so that they "catch" the "tail" of yarn. Secure the last couple of inches of yarn on the back of the work by running it under several stitches—horizontally or vertically, not diagonally.

When working with two strands of yarn, you can avoid having to hold the ends at the back when you begin by following this method: Take only one *thread* of yarn and fold it in half, ends together. Then, near the ends, thread the needle as you normally do—which is to lower the needle eye over the folded yarn pinched between your fingers, releasing the fold into the eye. Insert the needle through the back of the canvas where your first stitch will begin, then pull up, leaving a little of the loop at the back; then, as you insert the needle from the front of the canvas through to the back to complete the first stitch, put it through the loop and draw it through completely. You will then have secured the yarn very neatly.

The following is a general guide to the number of threads of Persian yarn to be used with each gauge of canvas when working a particular stitch, and to the appropriate size of tapestry needle:

(A) Three threads, #18 needle, on 10-mesh-to-the-inch canvas
or
Two threads, #20 or #22 needle, on 12-, 13-, or 14-mesh-to-the-inch canvas

> Basketweave
> Continental
> Mosaic
> Cashmere
> Knitting
> Scotch

(B) Three threads, #20 needle, on 12-, 13-, or 14-mesh-to-the-inch canvas

> Straight Gobelin

(C) One thread, #22 needle, on 17-mesh-to-the-inch canvas

> Basketweave
> Continental

(The other stitches under (A) would fill in as well on 17-mesh canvas, but they are not very effective on this small a scale.)

If you wish to work a particular design on canvas with a greater number of mesh per inch to produce a smaller finished piece, or on canvas of fewer mesh per inch for a larger piece, follow this procedure:

Divide the number of mesh per inch you are using into the total number of mesh or holes the design covers, for each dimension. This will give you, in inches, the length and width of the design area needed to work the design. You must then add at least an extra two inches for each dimension to allow for an unworked margin of canvas. In some cases, you will note that working on 10-mesh-to-the-inch canvas a cushion design that was originally intended for 17-mesh-to-the-inch canvas would result in an inordinately large cushion; similarly, the reverse would result in quite a tiny cushion. Therefore, usually, a change in canvas gauge should be to a number of mesh fairly close to the original number, such as 10 to 12, or possibly 14, and vice versa. Remember that enlarging the design will require using more yarn—you will need about one third more when changing from 14-mesh-to-the-inch to 10, about one third less when changing from 10 to 14.

NOTE: If you are accustomed to purchasing your Persian yarns by the ounce, count on about 40 yards to the ounce. If you buy by the cut strand, be sure these are in yard lengths; if they are shorter you will have to compensate and buy more of them.

Working with Light-Colored Yarns:

White and other very light colors have a tendency to show the tiny fibers of other strong colors, especially red, when light-colored yarn is drawn across worked areas. The effect amounts to tinting the white yarn; for example, it turns pink when drawn across a red area. In general, it's best to work light areas first, then medium, then dark. Also, unless your fingers are *perfectly* clean, worked white yarn will tend to look soiled and have an uneven appearance in large areas. To avoid this, clean your fingers again with a cotton ball dampened with rubbing alcohol after washing your hands.

Metallic Yarn:

For the designs in this book that feature metallic yarns, I recommend Bucilla Spotlight. This yarn comes on a 130-yard spool; you will cut the yarn into 12- to 14-inch lengths to keep it from fraying. One strand works very well on 12-, 13-, or 14-mesh-to-the-inch canvas; two threads (one strand doubled over) work well on 10-mesh-to-the-inch canvas. This metallic yarn is chained from many fine filaments to form the strand, rather than plied as Persian yarn is. Therefore care must be taken when it is used single-thread to prepare the end that passes in and out of the canvas to keep it from unraveling:

Cut the yarn into lengths and lay them out on a piece of waxed paper. Prepare one end of each strand by applying *old* nail polish about a quarter of an inch up. Before it has dried, roll the end between your fingers to make the enamel penetrate the strand. All this may seem a bit of a bother, but the effect of metallic yarn is really stunning.

If you use two threads on 10-mesh-to-the-inch canvas, preparing the ends will not be necessary: Thread the needle as you would with sewing thread, using a strand as long as 24 inches; fold the strand over, ends together and needle at the fold. Then hold an inch or so of the two ends at the back of the canvas, inserting the needle through the back to the front of the canvas. Begin to stitch, "anchoring" the ends as you work. The particular designs in this book that call for metallic yarn, however, are to be worked on 14-mesh-to-the-inch canvas, so don't throw out that sticky old nail polish!

Following the Graphs

Most of these weaving designs are to be worked using the basic stitches—Basketweave or Continental; therefore, in most cases, the small grid squares (not the lines) of the graphs represent *mesh* of canvas to be *covered* by the stitches. This also applies to the graphs of designs where the Knitting stitch is called for; in this case, the outlined areas denote (1) the first of the two canvas mesh crossed by the *first* Knitting stitch of a particular color and (2) the first of the two canvas mesh crossed by the *last* Knitting stitch of that color in the row being worked. Therefore, the *last* canvas mesh crossed by the last Knitting stitch of that color will be the same mesh, crossed *below*, as that crossed *above* by the first Knitting stitch of the adjacent color. (Please refer to the stitch diagrams, pages 27–29; they say all of this much better.)

The small grid squares (not lines) also represent mesh of canvas covered by Mosaic, Cashmere, or Scotch stitches when the design calls for any of these, as they are essentially variations of the basic stitches.

When the straight Gobelin stitch is required for a design, the graph illustrates the procedure in two ways:

In the first instance, as for the graphs for the "Liley of the West" cushion **(3)** and for the Ashanti *kente*-cloth cushion **(39)**, the small grid squares represent the vertical *mesh adjacent* to the holes which are *hidden* by the stitch. In other words, four vertical color-marked small grid squares on the graph for the "Liley of the West" cushion represent mesh lying between two straight Gobelin stitches *five holes high*, each hiding four holes. (Please refer to the stitch diagrams on pages 27–29; they also illustrate this relation of stitch to holes and mesh much better than words do.)

In the second instance, the small grid squares represent *holes* where the straight Gobelin stitches begin and end, and holes between these hidden by the stitches. The lines of the graph, therefore, represent the mesh of the canvas. This use of the graph occurs only once, to illustrate the stitching of the "John Madison" cushion.

When following a graph that represents only a quarter of the design, it may be simplest to start at the upper right-hand corner, complete this quarter, and then reverse the direction of the pattern with each remaining quarter (see ON SYMMETRY). However, you may prefer to begin at the center (marked C or indicated by a "+," "×," or "o," as specified in the directions); complete a section of the pattern in the quarter given, and then work the same section in reverse in each succeeding quarter.

Where the graph represents half of the design or the entire design, this indicates that the design is not one of radial symmetry, and it may be best to begin at the upper right-hand corner. You may choose to work certain areas of the design first, such as linear areas, in order to outline sections that then can be filled in easily.

Before you begin to work from any of the graphs, please read the section ON SYMMETRY.

If you find it more pleasurable to work a painted or marked canvas—rather than following the graph as you stitch a blank canvas—here are some notes on transferring a pattern from the graph to the canvas:

You will find water-base acrylic paints very convenient; they dry very quickly so that you may freely brace your forearm against already-painted areas in order to paint counted areas with precision. In general, they are very reliable and will not "run" onto the yarn when blocked with cold water, but, as an extra precaution, I always "set" my painted canvases with a clear acrylic spray enamel—*not* a fixative designed to protect charcoal drawings. You may also use oil paints, but these are not as convenient when one is painting very precise, counted designs, as they take much longer to dry. If you do use oil paints, take care to thin them with turpentine to such a consistency that they will be thick enough to adhere to the canvas and not "bleed," yet thin enough so that they will dry completely in a day or two. Again, setting the painted surface with acrylic spray when it is completely dry is advisable.

On the other hand, if you have no familiarity with paints at all, you will find very helpful some permanent fine-line markers, such as Nēpo markers (see SOURCES), made specifically for needlepoint. These come in several colors plus black. Simply outline with the black marker the spaces between the mesh to be covered with a particular color of yarn. Then you may note each color with a "scribble" from the colored marker that approximates it. Or, knot short pieces of each appropriate yarn color into the appropriate outlined areas.

Designing Your Own Canvas

Once you have become comfortable with the process of transferring a graphed design to canvas by means of paints or markers, the next step might be to consider designing a canvas from your own woven-design source. This is not as difficult as it may seem. It does not require any drawing ability, as woven patterns tend to be geometric and to make a graceful transition onto needlepoint canvas. What this kind of designing does require is something of an analytical turn of mind and, at times, patience, as when a pattern requires considerable adjusting to transpose it to the medium of needlepoint. In certain cases, a "stubborn streak" (or, if you prefer, determination) comes in very handy.

But, often enough, a woven pattern can be directly transcribed to canvas with little or no adjustment, especially when there are few angles. Oblique angles, such as those found in the Turkmenian cushion **(48)**, are tricky, but note that rendering them "believable" in needlepoint is simply a matter of finding the right sequence of "steps" or indentations along the rows of canvas mesh to achieve the illusion of the angle desired.

A large textile woven to be used as a carpet, blanket, or wraparound often has many design elements or a complicated design structure. Don't let this throw you. Consider it an intriguing challenge to find an area that will be adaptable to the scale of the canvas gauge you wish to use and the size of the object you have in mind. Or, conversely, calculate how to adjust your choice of canvas gauge and overall size to suit the design you've chosen, to adapt. Also, consider any area of a pattern with reference to the quality of the composition that will result when it is confined within the square or rectangle of needlepoint canvas. Usually, the perception of some form of symmetry (see the following section ON SYMMETRY) is most preferred. But often an overall diagonal structure, such as in the Peruvian tray design **(17)**, gives an effect more of movement across the surface—at least as appealing as the sometimes static effect of symmetrical structure.

When considering color, bear in mind that the beautiful textiles you find in museums were conceived and usually executed by artists—although perhaps not celebrated or self-conscious to the degree painters and sculptors usually are in our culture. Therefore, the particular color harmony of an exceptional textile, as well as its design structure, will have a "rhyme and reason" that we should open ourselves to, even though, at first glance, the use of color typical of other cultures may be disturbing. As with other cultural ideas and institutions, we often find that craftsmen of other civilizations have known what they were doing for a long time. So, try not to be shy of the unusual or "exotic"; do trust the pleasurable sensation you may experience, in spite of our cultural prohibitions against certain combinations of color in the name of "taste." On the other hand, don't be afraid to change the colors of a woven design to suit yourself; it's nobody's business but your own. Enjoy yourself!

In my research for the designs in this book, I have found working at the various museums very pleasant. The museum people were kind and helpful, making available to me textiles not on current exhibition and suggesting specific pieces that might be particularly appropriate for this project. I am sure you will find that museums in your area will have in their collections beautiful textiles that you may adapt for your own designs. Make inquiries and I'm sure you will find the museum people glad to be of assistance. Also, where many textiles are on exhibition, you can always sit in front of a display case and work out your chosen design on graph paper, even putting in the colors with felt-tip markers.

For some designs, you will find it possible and desirable to make use of different needlepoint stitches to simulate the texture of the original weaving—as I have done in the cases of the "Liley of the West" cushion (3) and the Ashanti *kente*-cloth cushion (39). The straight Gobelin stitch produces the ridged effect of weft threads passing over and under warp threads, especially in tapestry weaving; this also resembles the long "floating" threads in overshot weaving. The Knitting stitch bears a resemblance to the Soumak technique found in some Oriental carpets and American Indian weaving. Other stitches, such as the Mosaic, Cashmere, and Scotch stitches, while not imitating woven effects, often enliven the surface and add interest to a basically simple design.

I hope you will be adventurous and give designing your own canvas a try. It can be very satisfying to do and an opportunity to bring into your environment designs that have a special meaning for you.

On Symmetry

In working any of the designs in this book, it will be very helpful if you understand the type of symmetry on which each one is based. The photographs accompanying the graphs should serve to make this clear, but, when in doubt, refer to these notes on the subject:

The type of symmetry most often found in the designs is *radial symmetry*, in which the arrangement of the pattern is the same in each of the four quarters, except that the sequence reverses direction from one quarter to the next, as in a mirror image. An example of this type is the Bulgarian cushion, central diamond motif **(30)**. The "Blooming Leaf" cushion **(1)** is another example of this type of symmetry; however, executing this one will be easier, as the entire reverse in sequence takes place within the quarter given in the graph and the remaining three quarters are simply repeated. Another example of radial symmetry is the Shirvan cushion **(47)**; in this case, though, the entire design is represented in the graph because of the color changes that occur in the repeated motifs.

The second type of symmetry you will find among these designs is *horizontal-axis symmetry*, as in the Iroquois "Lightning" cushion **(7)**. In this case, the entire upper half of the design is reversed in the lower half. The Navajo "Arrows" cushion **(6)** represents a variation of this type in that the sequence of the pattern reverses only partly in the lower half. The Moro cushion **(59)** is not an example of this type of symmetry, as the lower half of the design is an exact repetition of the upper half, with no change of direction or color at all.

The third type, *vertical-axis symmetry*, occurs only in the instance of the Turkmenian cushion **(48)**, where the left half of the design reflects the right half, reversing direction.

Blocking

Blocking can be a much simpler matter than you might think, especially if you primarily have used the Basketweave stitch in working your design; the Continental stitch, if used extensively, will distort your canvas much more and will probably require several blockings. The other stitches described in the diagrams included in this book do not distort the canvas; they require only that you steam the canvas on the back side with your iron set at "wool" or "synthetic" temperature, placing a wrung-out wet terry cloth between iron and canvas. (The Knitting stitch tends to pull in the canvas slightly, causing the horizontal dimension to be a little shorter than it was originally; therefore this stitch is not advisable for working prefinished articles.)

To restore a distorted canvas to its original square or rectangular dimensions, here is what you do: Mark a large wooden board with a grid of one-inch squares, using a heavy permanent and waterproof marker and a ruler. Have a bowl of cold water and a pristine sponge on hand, and wet the canvas thoroughly by pressing the wet sponge into the work from the back, saturating it through to the front of the canvas. Then, with the canvas face up, line up an edge of it with a grid line on your board, which you will be able to see through the unworked margins of the canvas. With a staple gun, secure the canvas with staples fairly close together in the margin. You can then ease the other side of the canvas into position, following the appropriate grid lines on the board, so that the piece is restored to its original dimensions. The canvas will require a couple of days to dry; then, pry up the staples with a screwdriver.

Finishing

When it comes to finishing, I must rely on the skills of people who specialize in finishing cushions, upholstering furniture, and framing wall hangings. But here are some things to be aware of, whether you have professionals do your finishing work for you or are able to do it yourself:

A skillful seamstress or upholsterer is usually able to attach backing fabric to a needlepoint canvas to make a cushion without sacrificing any of the worked area along the edges, and to apply a corded edge at the same time. Check this out, preferably before you begin to work your canvas; if it turns out that your favorite person for this job must take up a few rows of the worked area in the seam allowance, you will have to add extra rows rather than lose them. A convenient feature you might request is a zipper sewn into the backing so you will be able to remove the separate inner pillow for flat dry-cleaning of the needlepoint. Unless your needlepoint canvas is a square larger than 16 or 17 inches both ways, a half yard of backing fabric should be sufficient, allowing a large remaining area from which diagonal strips for the corded edge may be cut and pieced together. I have found ribless corduroy, which has a velvety look, to be a fine backing material as it is available in many colors compatible with these designs and is priced very reasonably. Velvet, of course, is very elegant, and so are the synthetic suede-type fabrics. Linens and synthetic linen-type fabrics are also fine and are available in many bright colors.

A good framer should need to take up very little of the work around the edges of your needlepoint canvas in attaching it to the board or stretchers that will support the frame you have chosen. And, speaking of frames, generally the simplest frame is best for needlepoint, as any attention other than to the design itself should be drawn to the stitchery, not to the intricacies of an ornamental frame. On the other hand, a very severe frame, such as a chrome molding, will not suit every design, especially not one of a particularly delicate character.

In upholstering your needlepoint to a piece of furniture, your professional should first be able to block large pieces for you. Before embarking upon a project such as re-covering a chair, for instance, you can request your upholsterer to make templates from the areas you will be re-covering—seat, back, arms—in order to transfer the shapes and dimensions to the needlepoint canvas correctly. If you make the templates yourself, use large-size brown wrapping paper or tissue for each one, and pin it to the piece of furniture. Feel the edge of the shape of the piece through the paper, and use a pencil to draw along it. Remove the paper and then add at least an extra inch past your outline. Your upholsterer will need the extra worked canvas to ease the piece over rounded surfaces and to take it under at the edges. See the Iranian Kirman chair-cover design **(43)** for more detailed instructions.

The Stitches

These are the stitches called for most often in the designs in this book. The Basketweave and the Continental look much the same on the front of the work, but the Basketweave is usually the better stitch to use, as it does not distort the canvas as much as does the Continental and you do not have to turn the canvas upside down as you do when working alternate rows of Continental. The Basketweave stitch does, however, require more yarn than the Continental.

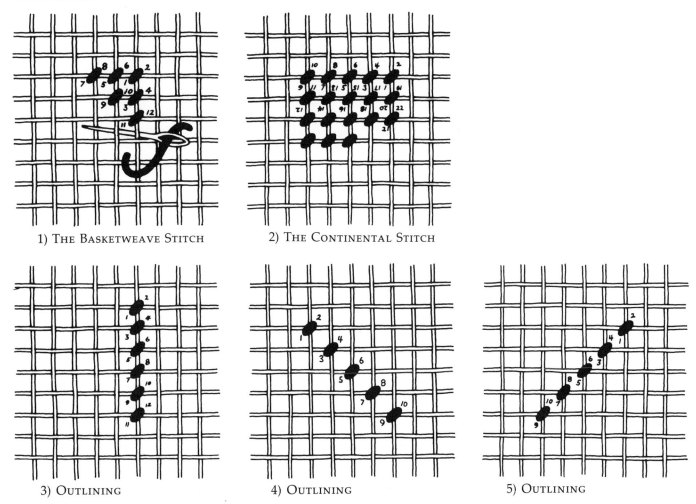

1) THE BASKETWEAVE STITCH

2) THE CONTINENTAL STITCH

3) OUTLINING

4) OUTLINING

5) OUTLINING

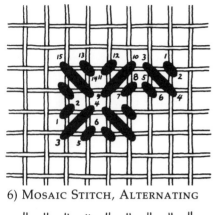

6) Mosaic Stitch, Alternating

As you may perceive, the Mosaic stitch is a variation of the basic stitch, and the Cashmere and Scotch are only further variations of the Mosaic stitch. A decided advantage to working these stitches alternating the direction, as they are represented here, is that they will not distort the canvas. Since I discovered this for myself, I've never been inclined to work them repeating the same direction; the effect is more interesting, anyway, when they alternate. If you find these stitches fun to work, stitching the "Wandering Vine" rug **(4)** will be a big treat, as all of these are used for that design.

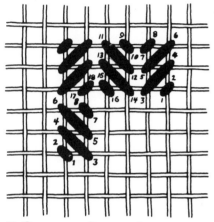

7) Cashmere Stitch, Alternating

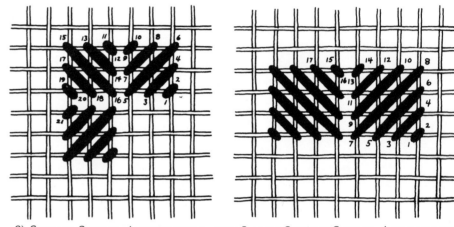

8) Scotch Stitch, Alternating, and Large Scotch Stitch, Alternating

This stitch produces a handsome, "shimmering" effect. It seems easy to maintain an even tension with it and, therefore, to achieve a consistent look to the work. It is to be worked horizontally; therefore, in working the West African cushion **(40)**, which features the stitch both horizontally and vertically, you will turn the canvas on its side to work the areas that appear vertical.

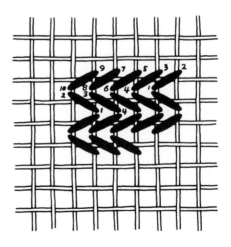

9) Knitting Stitch

A great variety of effects can be achieved with this stitch, depending on the height of the stitch used, whether or not you use different heights of the stitch in the piece, and whether or not you use it both vertically and horizontally. To work this stitch horizontally, you do not have to turn the canvas. Three heights (indicating the number of canvas *holes* high) are given in this diagram—from 3 holes high to 5 holes high; or, *adjacent* to 2 to 4 mesh of canvas, if you prefer to think of it this way. This stitch may also be worked 6 holes high, as it is in the "John Madison" cushion **(2)**.

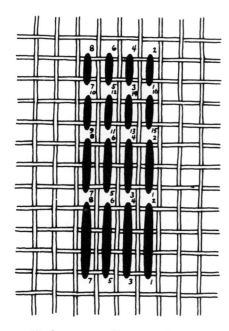

10) STRAIGHT GOBELIN STITCH

The Designs

Early American Designs

1. "Blooming Leaf" Cushion

17 1/2" × 13 1/2"—Color Plates Pages 66, 67

The pattern for this design was derived from an American handwoven textile of the type known as "Diamonds." This and the following three traditional patterns were found in *A Handweaver's Pattern Book* by Marguerite Porter Davison, an extensive and fascinating collection of patterns for the four-harness loom.

CANVAS: 10 mesh to the inch. Design covers 177 mesh horizontally by 137 mesh vertically; a piece of canvas at least 19 1/2" by 15 1/2" will be sufficient.

NEEDLE: #18

YARNS: Use the full strand of Persian yarn in the following amounts:
1) white, 110 yds.
2) medium seafoam green, 130 yds.
3) dark seafoam green, 120 yds.

STITCH: Basketweave

NOTE: An *x* marks the center of the design, which falls on a mesh of canvas. The other three *x*'s indicate where the entire pattern repeats.

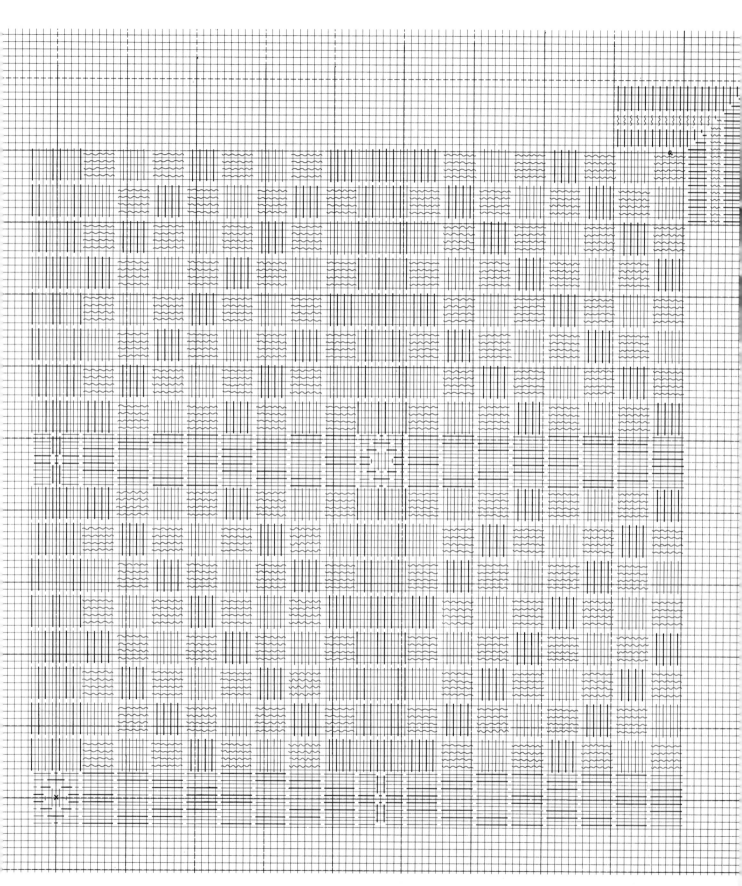

2. "John Madison" Cushion

14 1/4" × 14 1/4"—COLOR PLATE PAGE 67

Many of the American coverlet patterns produce a striking optical effect, as appealing to the modern sensibility as they were in the colonial period. One of these, the "John Madison" pattern, is adapted here to be worked in a Bargello type of stitch, the straight Gobelin.

CANVAS: 14 mesh to the inch. Design spans a 200-*hole* square; a square of canvas at least 16 1/4" by 16 1/4" will be sufficient.

NEEDLE: #20

YARNS: Use the full strand of Persian yarn in the following amounts:

1) yellowish white, 40 yds.
2) medium bright gold, 50 yds.
3) dark bright gold, 60 yds.

STITCH: Straight Gobelin stitch, in varying heights, spanning two to six holes, worked both vertically and horizontally.

NOTE: In this graph, the small grid squares represent *holes* and the lines represent *mesh*. A good way to establish the pattern is to work the eight sets of four Gobelins each, in medium gold, beginning at *a*. Work the remaining medium-gold sets in this area; then fill in the vertical white and dark-gold sets. Work the "cross" pattern, then work the remaining square areas around it. Continue in this manner to complete the design; finish by working the borders. IMPORTANT: Separate each strand of yarn into its three threads and hold them all together while working, in order to achieve the fullness you will need; the canvas will peek through slightly, but the impact of the pattern will overpower this.

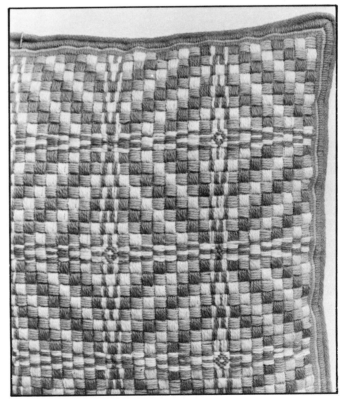

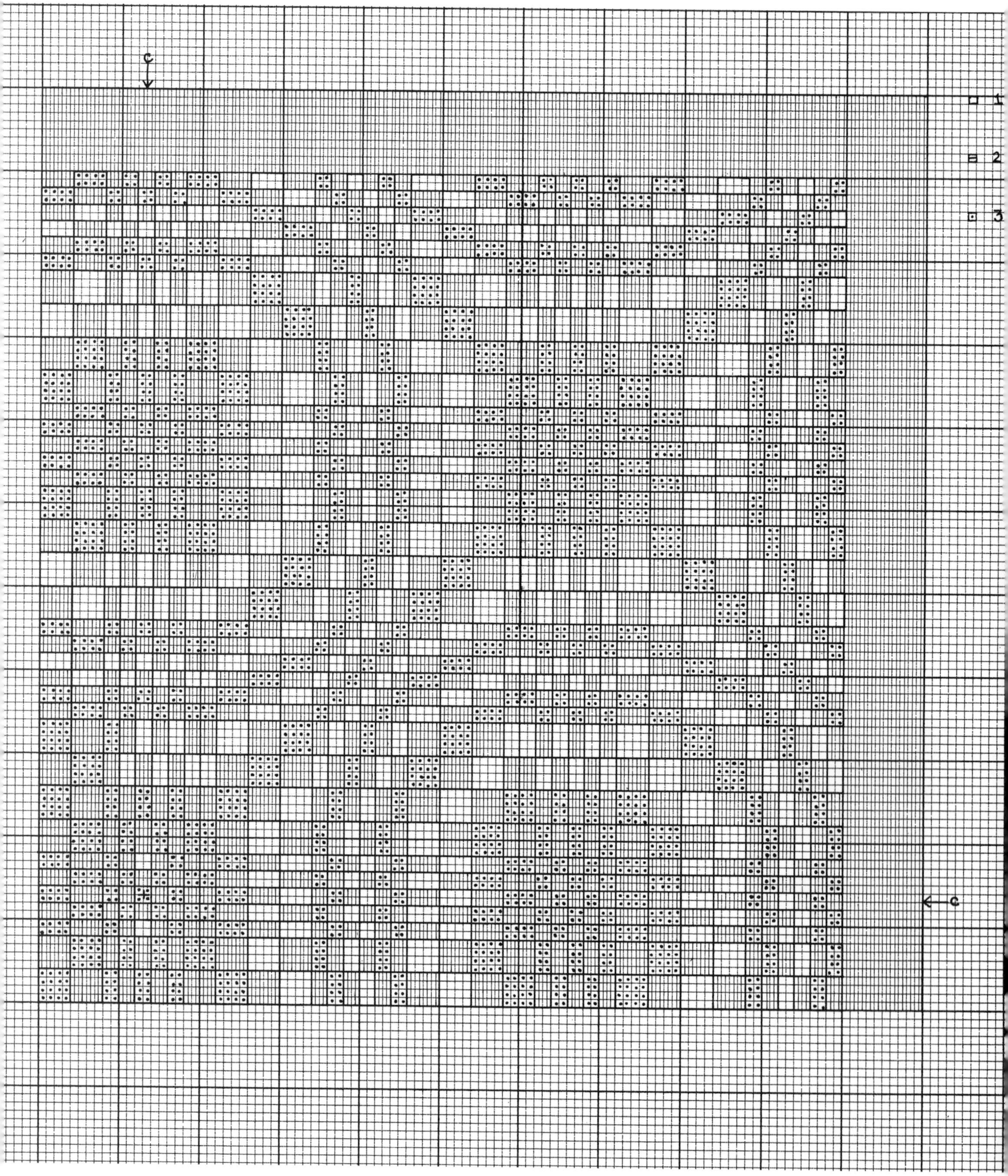
c
1
2
3
c

3. "Liley of the West" Cushion

14″ × 14″—COLOR PLATE PAGE 67

Another colonial pattern inspired the design for this piece. As with the other coverlet patterns, shades of almost any color would be very handsome.

CANVAS: 14 mesh to the inch. Design spans a 195-*hole* square; a square of canvas at least 16″ by 16″ will be sufficient.
NEEDLE: #20
YARNS: Use the full strand of Persian yarn in the following amounts:
1) light Federal blue, 50 yds.
2) medium Federal blue, 90 yds.
3) dark Federal blue, 40 yds.
STITCH: Straight Gobelin stitch, two heights—three holes high and five holes high—worked vertically only.

NOTE: The small grid squares of the graph represent the *mesh* of canvas adjacent to the holes *hidden* by the stitch. Therefore, a Gobelin three holes high lies adjacent to *two* canvas *mesh*, and a Gobelin five holes high lies adjacent to *four* canvas *mesh*. A "+" marks the center mesh of your canvas.

A good way to establish the pattern is to follow these steps: Leave the border for the very last. At the upper right-hand corner of the canvas (leaving room for the border), work the first two dark-blue Gobelins, then continue working each set of two or four Gobelins diagonally down to the center, which will lie between a pair of short Gobelins. Then work all of the medium sets of the upper right quarter of the design, represented by the graph. The rest will then be a matter of filling in the remaining light-blue and dark-blue sets between the medium sets. Work the other three quarters of the design by reversing the sequence (refer to photo). Finish by working the border in medium blue, as follows: Side borders will be ten Gobelins out from the edge of the

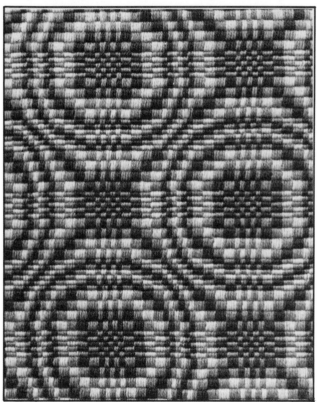

pattern, continuing alongside the worked Gobelins; each row of ten border Gobelins down the side will be the same height as the pattern Gobelins in that row. Top and bottom borders will each be five rows of Gobelins three holes high, and will span the width defined by the side borders.

4. "Wandering Vine" Rug

25 1/4" × 37 1/4"—Color Plate Page 67

The large overshot pattern also called "Snail's Trail" and "Cat Track" inspired the design for this rug. The curving outer lines of the pattern are modified to create a waving border effect.

CANVAS: 10 mesh to the inch. Design covers 252 mesh horizontally by 372 mesh vertically; a piece of canvas at least 27 1/4" by 39 1/4" will be sufficient.

NEEDLE: #18

YARNS: Use the full strand of Persian yarn in the following amounts:
1) light bright gold, 180 yds.
2) medium bright gold, 480 yds. (plus 320 yds. for fringe and binding stitch)
3) dark bright gold, 290 yds.

STITCHES: Mosaic stitch, alternating
   Cashmere stitch, alternating
   Scotch stitch, alternating, large variation

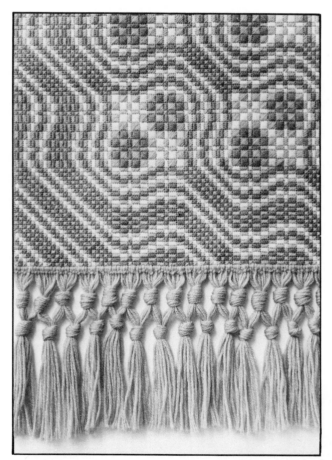

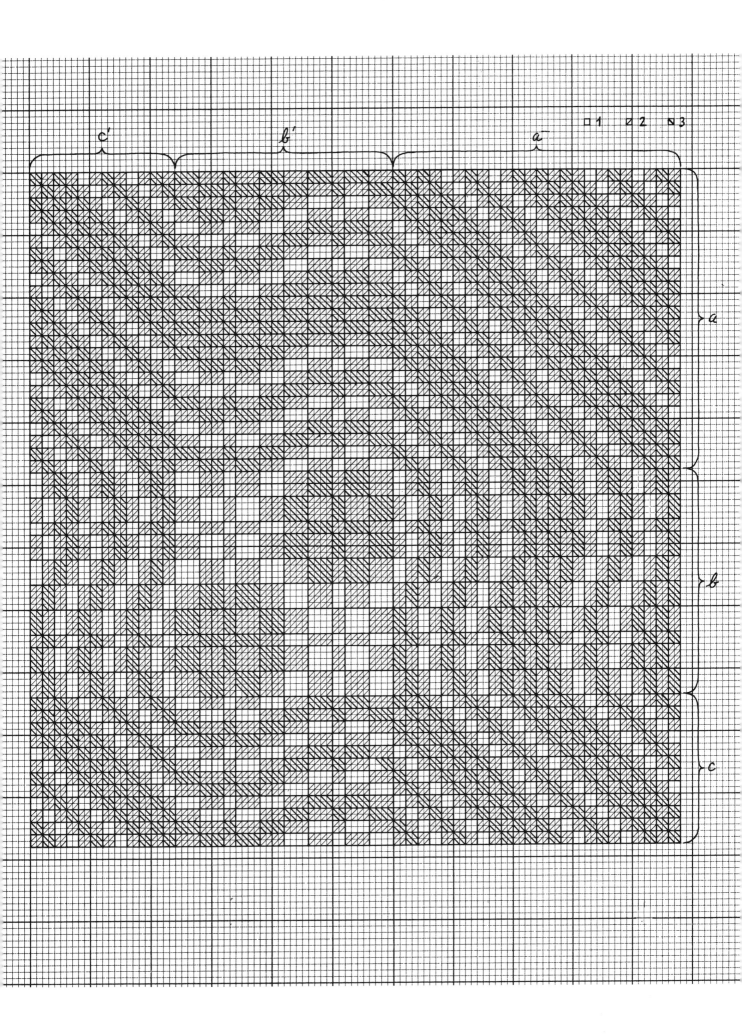

a	b1	c1	b1	c1	b1	a
b	$\frac{b1}{b}$	$\frac{c1}{b}$	$\frac{b1}{b}$	$\frac{c1}{b}$	$\frac{b1}{b}$	b
c	$\frac{b1}{c}$	$\frac{c1}{c}$	$\frac{b1}{c}$	$\frac{c1}{c}$	$\frac{b1}{c}$	c
b	$\frac{b1}{b}$	$\frac{c1}{b}$	$\frac{b1}{b}$	$\frac{c1}{b}$	$\frac{b1}{b}$	b
c	$\frac{b1}{c}$	$\frac{c1}{c}$	$\frac{b1}{c}$	$\frac{c1}{c}$	$\frac{b1}{c}$	c
b	$\frac{b1}{b}$	$\frac{c1}{b}$	$\frac{b1}{b}$	$\frac{c1}{b}$	$\frac{b1}{b}$	b
c	$\frac{b1}{c}$	$\frac{c1}{c}$	$\frac{b1}{c}$	$\frac{c1}{c}$	$\frac{b1}{c}$	c
b	$\frac{b1}{b}$	$\frac{c1}{b}$	$\frac{b1}{b}$	$\frac{c1}{b}$	$\frac{b1}{b}$	b
c	$\frac{b1}{c}$	$\frac{c1}{c}$	$\frac{b1}{c}$	$\frac{c1}{c}$	$\frac{b1}{c}$	c
b	$\frac{b1}{b}$	$\frac{c1}{b}$	$\frac{b1}{b}$	$\frac{c1}{b}$	$\frac{b1}{b}$	b
c	$\frac{b1}{c}$	$\frac{c1}{c}$	$\frac{b1}{c}$	$\frac{c1}{c}$	$\frac{b1}{c}$	c
b	$\frac{b1}{b}$	$\frac{c1}{b}$	$\frac{b1}{b}$	$\frac{c1}{b}$	$\frac{b1}{b}$	b
a	b1	c1	b1	c1	b1	a

NOTE: Follow the graph for the basic blocks, repeating these blocks as illustrated in the pattern diagram to complete the entire rug. You will not have to reverse any of the sequences yourself; note that section *b1* is a mirror image reverse of section *b*, etc. Also note that the four corner blocks, illustrated as section *a*, are nowhere reversed, in order to maintain the "flowing" effect of the pattern, rather than to give the effect of "containment" achieved when the corners of a border design reverse.

A photograph of the back side of one corner is given to demonstrate the lack of complication involved in finishing off such a rug. A very ingenious stitch was used to bind the edges of the design after it was folded over, matching rows of mesh along the fold. (See *Miracles with the Binding Stitch* under SOURCES.) If you wish to line the rug, you may use a suitable medium-weight fabric for this purpose. I have heard of a rubber-type coating which may be applied to the back of the rug to make it skid proof, but not having tried this myself, I cannot honestly recommend it. You might investigate this possibility for yourself, though. This particular rug will be used as a table covering, in the manner sometimes seen in Renaissance paintings.

The two shorter edges were fringed very effectively in the following manner: Approximately 32"-long strands of yarn were knotted along the unbound short edges about three for every four mesh, latch-hook style, resulting in twice as many ends, since they are doubled over. Add an extra strand about four times along each edge, evenly spaced, so that you will have inserted a number of strands divisible by eight. Then knot together the resulting doubled strands in groups of sixteen, fairly close to the edge. Separate the second knotted group in half and knot this half-group with the entire first group; continue along the edge, separating each group of sixteen strands and knotting eight from one group with eight from the next. You will knot the entire group at the end with the remaining half of the next-to-last group. This all may seem rather complicated in words, so do use the photograph in order to visualize more easily this basically simple process.

American Indian Designs

5. Navajo "Eye-Dazzler" Cushion

20" × 16"

As the name of this type of Navajo blanket design indicates, its pattern and coloring do combine to produce a dazzling effect. The design was adapted from a late-nineteenth-century blanket.

An interesting comment on this type of pattern comes from the catalog of the exhibition *The Navajo Blanket*, which I saw at the Brooklyn Museum in 1972: "As the Navajo culture moved from calm, complete self-confidence to total surrender and domination by a foreign culture, it was not at all surprising to find the emergence in the 1880s of an explosively 'expressionistic' style . . . the irradiating diamond was used to convey a level of energy and agitation that can only be termed expressionist, just as the plain-stripe style conveyed the essence of classical calm."

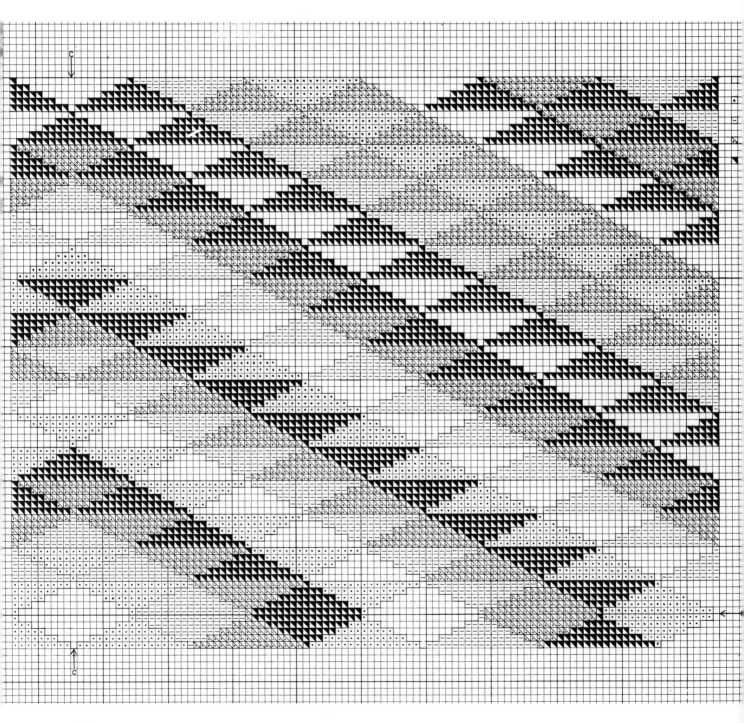

42

CANVAS: 10 mesh to the inch. Design covers 199 mesh horizontally by 160 mesh vertically; a piece of canvas at least 22″ by 18″ will be sufficient.

NEEDLE: #18

YARNS: Use the full strand of Persian yarn in the following amounts:

1) white, 55 yds.
2) bright yellow, 40 yds.
3) bright orange, 55 yds.
4) coral red, 70 yds.
5) black, 65 yds.

STITCH: Basketweave

6. Navajo "Arrows" Cushion

17 1/2″ × 16″—Color Plate Page 71

A banded saddle blanket inspired this design. Although the colors I have used here are not exactly typical of Navajo weaving, I chose them for the mellowing effect they have on the otherwise agitated quality of the pattern. Note the diminishing of the intensity of the yellow, from the middle band through the succeeding bands to the edges.

CANVAS: 14 mesh to the inch. The design covers 244 canvas mesh by 224 canvas mesh. A piece of canvas at least 19 1/2″ by 18″ will be sufficient.

NEEDLE: #22

YARNS: Separate Persian yarn and use two threads; you will need the following amounts before separating:

1) ivory, 95 yds.
2) bright golden yellow, 22 yds.
3) medium seafoam green, 75 yds.
4) bright rust, 80 yds.

STITCH: Knitting

NOTE: The small grid squares of this graph represent the *mesh* of canvas to be *covered* by the Knitting stitches. (See Following the Graphs, and refer to the stitch diagrams on pages 27–29.)

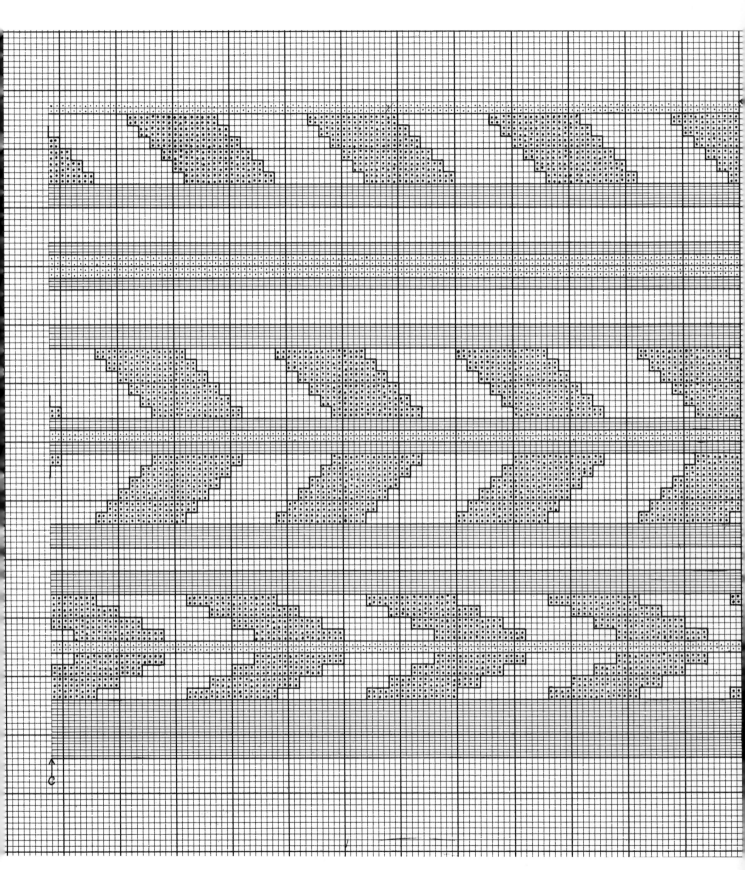

44

7. Iroquois "Lightning" Cushion

17″ × 16″—COLOR PLATE PAGE 71

A beautiful plaited sash of the type known as *ceinture flèchée*, now in the collection of the Peabody Museum, Cambridge, Massachusetts, provided the pattern for this design; the colors replicate those of the original.

CANVAS: 10 mesh to the inch. Design covers 167 mesh horizontally by 159 mesh vertically; a piece of canvas at least 19″ by 18″ will be sufficient.

NEEDLE: #18

YARNS: Use the full strand of Persian yarn in the following amounts:

1) white, 36 yds.
2) lemon yellow, 18 yds.
3) turquoise, 18 yds.
4) medium gray, 55 yds.
5) brick red, 110 yds.
6) black, 36 yds.

STITCH: Basketweave

NOTE: Work across graph A (page 46), continuing the established pattern over an equal number of canvas mesh beyond the vertical center mark, at top of graph. Continue, by working across graph B (page 47), to complete the lower half of the design, repeating the pattern to the left edge as with graph A.

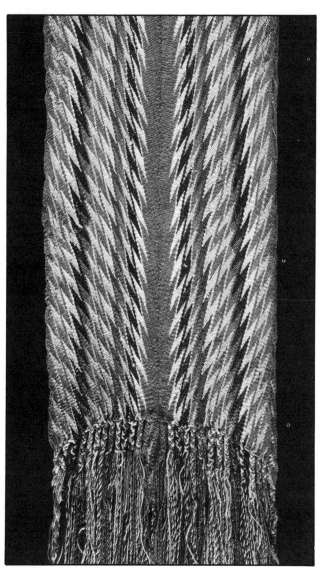

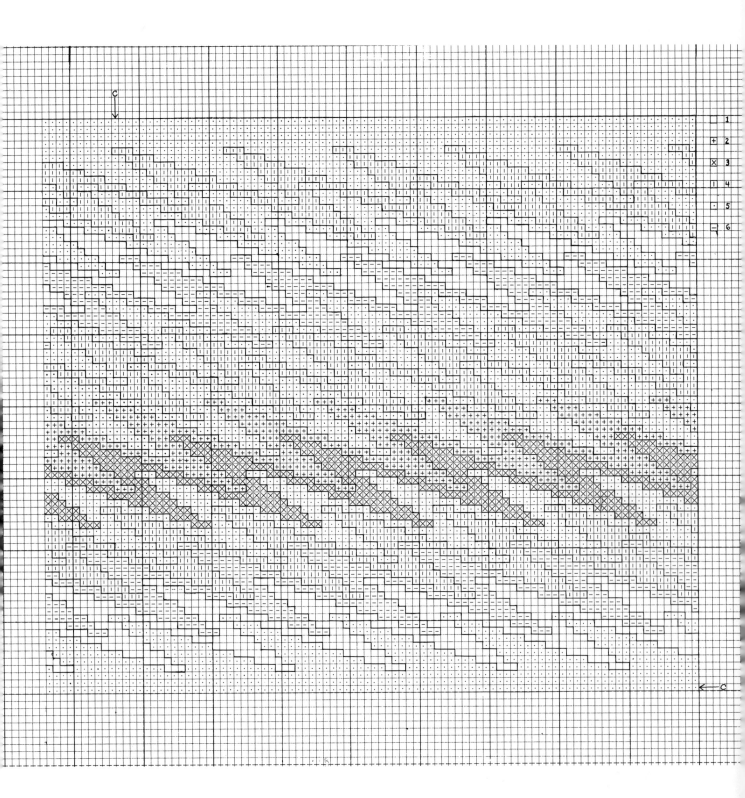

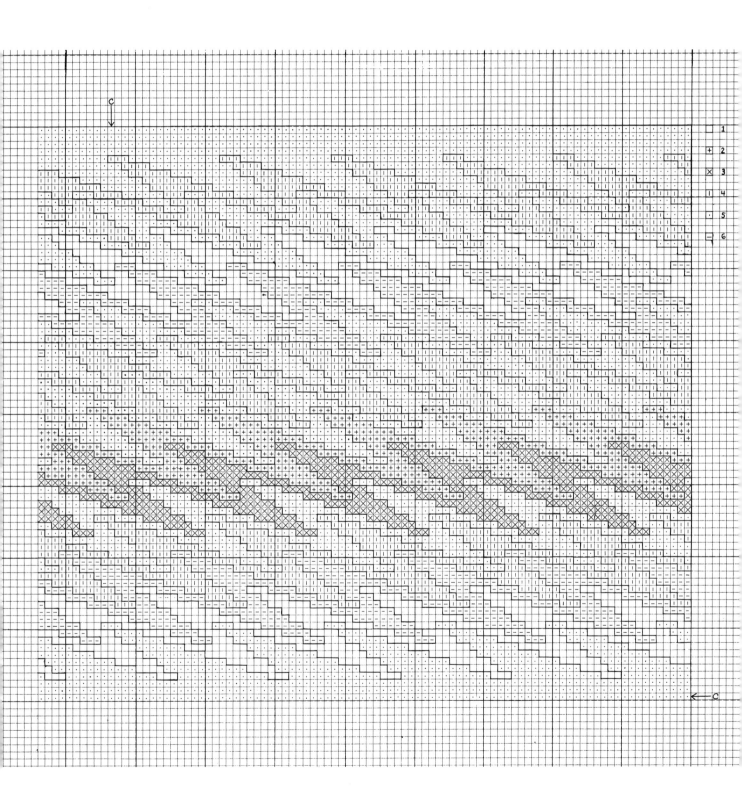

47

48

8. Hopi Wall Hanging

18 3/4" × 15 3/4"—COLOR PLATE PAGE 68

A ceremonial sash from Arizona, in the collection of the Peabody Museum, inspired this design. The sash is a particularly fine example of a typical style of Hopi textile; although over 45" long, it is only 9" wide, demonstrating the complexity of pattern, richness of color, and fineness of weave achieved by the Hopi in such a narrow field.

CANVAS: 13 mesh to the inch. Design covers 245 mesh horizontally by 205 mesh vertically; a piece of canvas at least 21" by 18" will be sufficient.

NEEDLE: #20 or #22

YARNS: Separate Persian yarns and use two threads; you will need the following amounts before separating:

1) white, 70 yds.
2) coral, 25 yds.
3) bright red, 6 yds.
4) jade green, 55 yds.
5) deep bright blue, 20 yds.
6) black, 75 yds.

STITCH: Continental

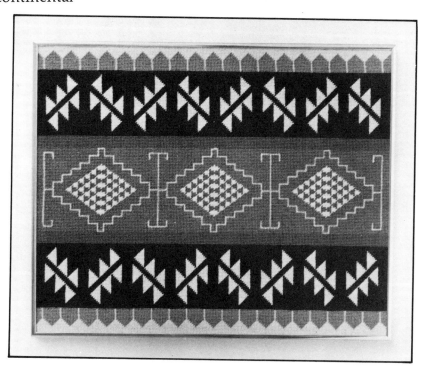

9. Dakota Cushion

16 1/2" × 15"—Color Plate Page 130

The pattern for this design and its unusual combination of colors derive from a beautiful Plains Indian textile in the collection of the Museum of Natural History, New York.

CANVAS: 10 mesh to the inch. Design covers 165 mesh horizontally by 150 mesh vertically; a piece of canvas at least 18 1/2" by 17" will be sufficient.

NEEDLE: #18

YARNS: Use the full strand of Persian yarn in the following amounts:

1) white, 100 yds.
2) light pink, 35 yds.
3) coral, 45 yds.
4) medium gray, 35 yds.
5) dark gray, 58 yds.
6) deep bright blue, 45 yds.

STITCH: Basketweave

NOTE: Following the graph, continue each band of the pattern an equal number of small grid squares past the center, not repeating the vertical center mesh. Work entire upper part of the design, completing the center band of triangles. Then follow the graph, beginning with the band directly above the center band, reversing the *order* of the bands as you work toward the lower edge of the design. *Do not* reverse the direction of the pattern within any of the bands. As with the upper part, continue the given sequence of each band past the center an equal number of small grid squares.

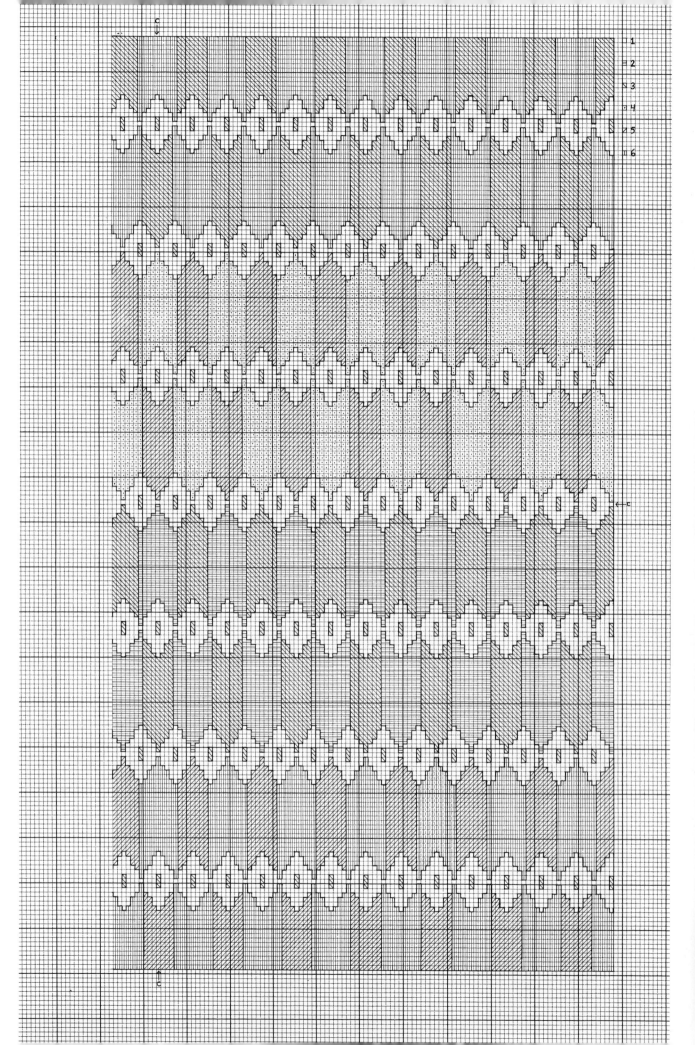

Central & South American Designs

10. Mexican Serape Cushion

15" × 15"—Color Plate Page 131

A Mexican serape inspired this design, one of a number of similar extraordinary pieces in the collection of the Peabody Museum. As in the original textile, the use of taupe intensifies the red and deep blue of the design; note how they change when they lie adjacent to the taupe.

CANVAS: 14 mesh to the inch. Design covers a 209-mesh square; a square of canvas at least 17" by 17" will be sufficient.
NEEDLE: #22
YARNS: Separate Persian yarn and use two threads; you will need the following amounts before separating:
1) white, 65 yds.
2) coral, 30 yds.
3) dark red, 55 yds.
4) light sky blue, 30 yds.
5) deep Delft blue, 55 yds.
6) medium taupe, 55 yds.
STITCH: Basketweave

NOTE: Continue each band of the design across an equal number of stitches past the center, without repeating the center vertical mesh.

11. Mexican Serape Design, Address-Book Cover

4″ × 5″—COLOR PLATE PAGE 131

The pattern of the preceding Mexican serape cushion was adapted to fit the cutout opening on the cover of this address book from Needlepoint, U.S.A. (see SOURCES). I chose a sand-colored cover to coordinate with the taupe of the design.

CANVAS: 14 mesh to the inch. Design covers 57 mesh horizontally by 71 mesh vertically; a piece of canvas 6″ by 7″ will be sufficient.

NEEDLE: #20 or #22

YARNS: Separate Persian yarn and use two threads; you will need the following amounts before separating:
1) white, 5 yds.
3) dark red, 5 yds.
5) deep Delft blue, 5 yds.
6) medium taupe, 9 yds.

STITCH: Basketweave

NOTE: See photo on page 75, illustrating the procedure for mounting a worked piece onto a cardboard backing (also supplied with address book). You can then lightly brush rubber cement onto the back of the cardboard and the cutout area of the address book; allow this to dry for a few minutes, then press the mounted piece into the cutout area.

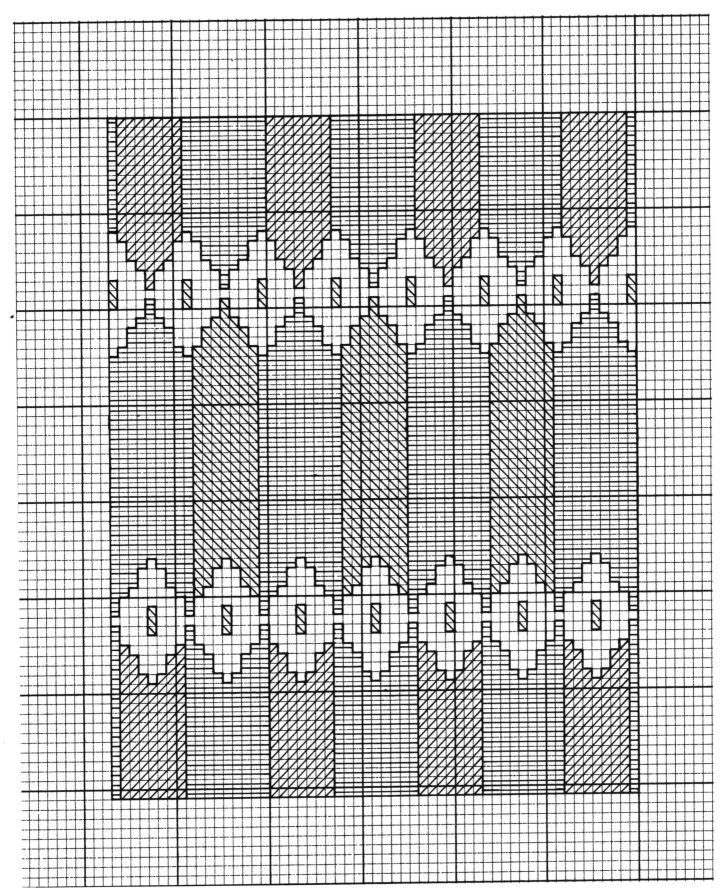

55

12. Guatemalan Wall Hanging

19″ × 28 1/2″—Color Plate Page 70

A modern brocade-weave textile from Guatemala inspired this wall hanging. I chose a deep brown for the ground color, but almost any color, even a light shade, would be suitable.

CANVAS: 10 mesh to the inch. Design (including plain border) covers 189 mesh horizontally by 285 mesh vertically; a piece of canvas at least 21″ by 30 1/2″ will be sufficient.

NEEDLE: #18

YARNS: Use the full strand of Persian yarn in the following amounts:
1) white, 350 yds.
2) deep brown, 200 yds.

STITCH: Basketweave

NOTE: Following the graph, repeat upper pattern band "a/b" three times, working toward the left edge; add one vertical row of pattern at end, to match the first such row along the right edge of graph. Similarly repeat pattern band "a/c" and "a/d." To finish lower part of design, repeat entire pattern band "a/c", then "a/b," after center band "a/d," not reversing the images, and adding the extra vertical row of pattern in each band at left edge.

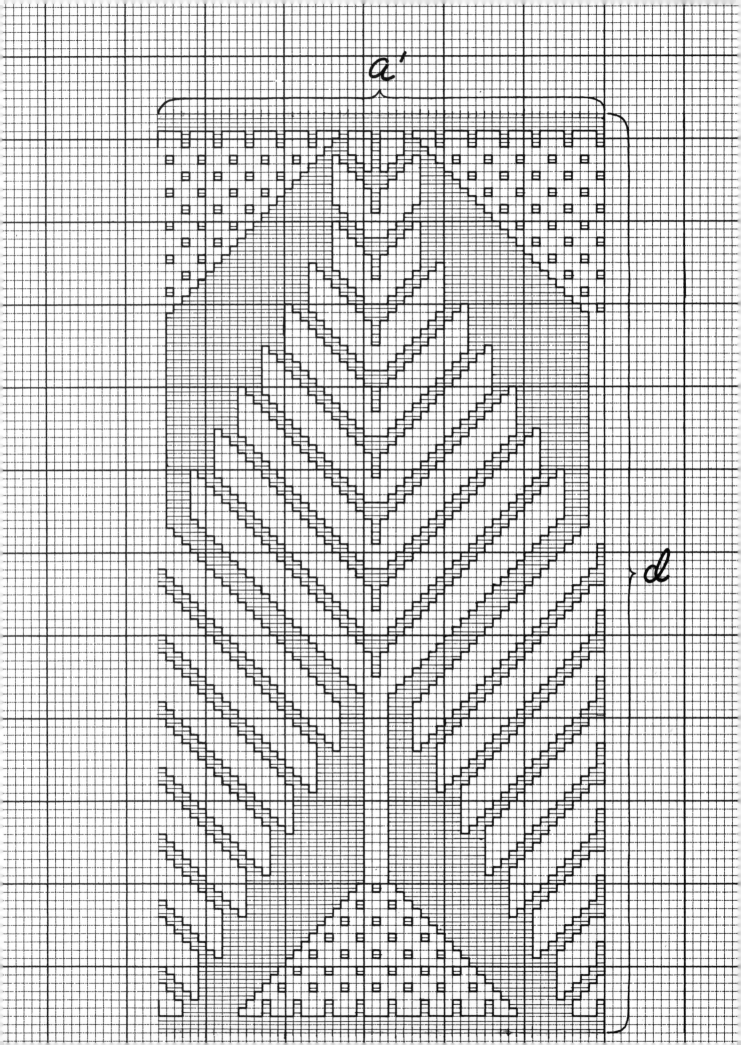

13. Guatemalan Design, Shoulder Bag

7 3/4″ × 6″ insert—COLOR PLATE PAGE 70

The pattern for this design is derived from an old-style ceremonial poncho of Totonicapán, Guatemala. I chose earthy tones for this piece rather than the more typical bright colors. The design was worked on a removable piece of canvas which is supplied with the leather shoulder bag made by Toni Totes of Vermont (see SOURCES).

CANVAS: 12 mesh to the inch. Design covers 99 mesh horizontally by 78 mesh vertically.

NEEDLE: #20 or #22

YARNS: Separate Persian yarn and use two threads; you will need the following amounts before separating:

1) white, 12 yds.
2) light taupe, 7 yds.
3) medium taupe, 10 yds.
4) medium bright gold, 6 yds.
5) medium rust, 8 yds.
6) dark brown, 5 yds.
7) black, 5 yds.

STITCH: Basketweave

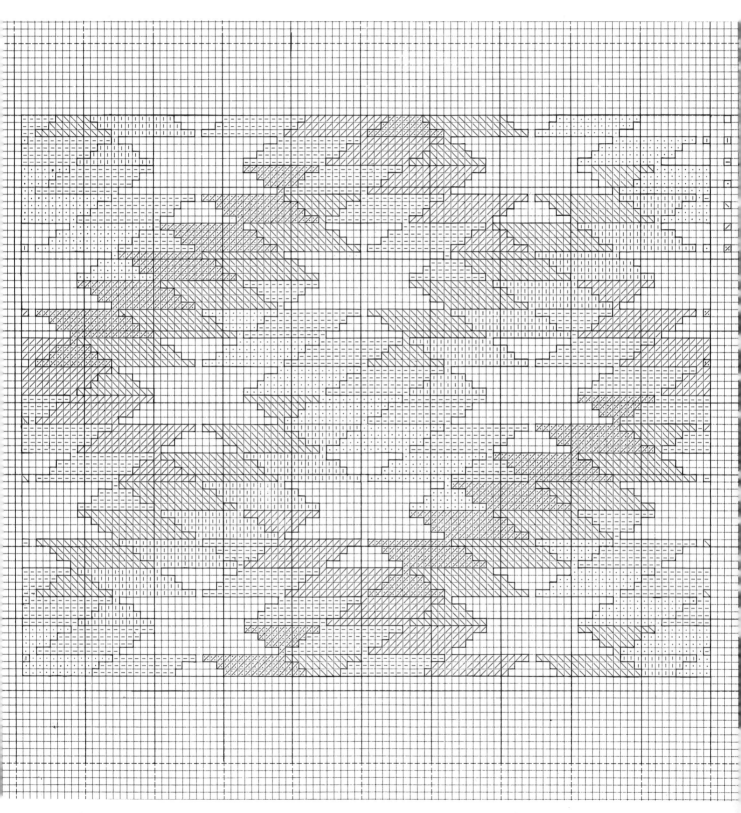

14. Inca Poncho Wall Hanging

15 3/4" × 15 3/4"—COLOR PLATE PAGE 69

The square motifs and border of this piece are adapted from several fifteenth-century Peruvian ponchos, all of a style typical of the period before the Spanish conquest. The colors derive from one of the ponchos.

CANVAS: 13 mesh to the inch. Design covers a 204-mesh square; a square of canvas at least 17 3/4" by 17 3/4" will be sufficient.

NEEDLE: #20 or #22

YARNS: Separate Persian yarn and use two threads; you will need the following amounts before separating:
1) white, 70 yds.
2) medium gold, 45 yds.
3) coral, 27 yds.
4) bright red, 27 yds.
5) deep bright blue, 25 yds.
6) black, 27 yds.

STITCHES: Basketweave and Scotch, alternating

NOTE: Work square motifs in Basketweave. Work border of each motif in Scotch stitch, alternating. Similarly, work the outer "checkered" border and two final white rows in Scotch stitch, alternating.

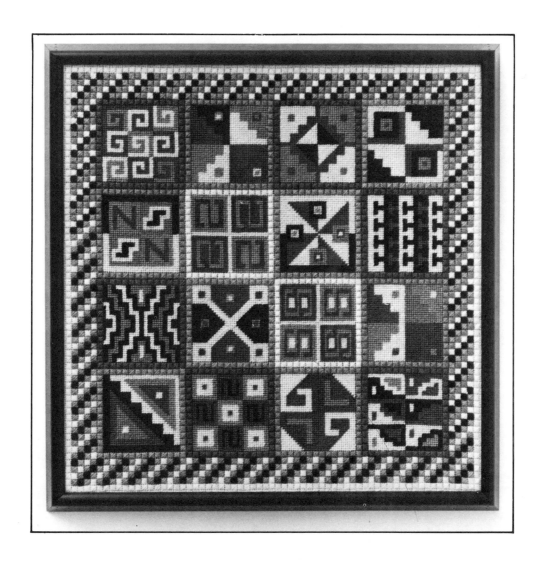

61

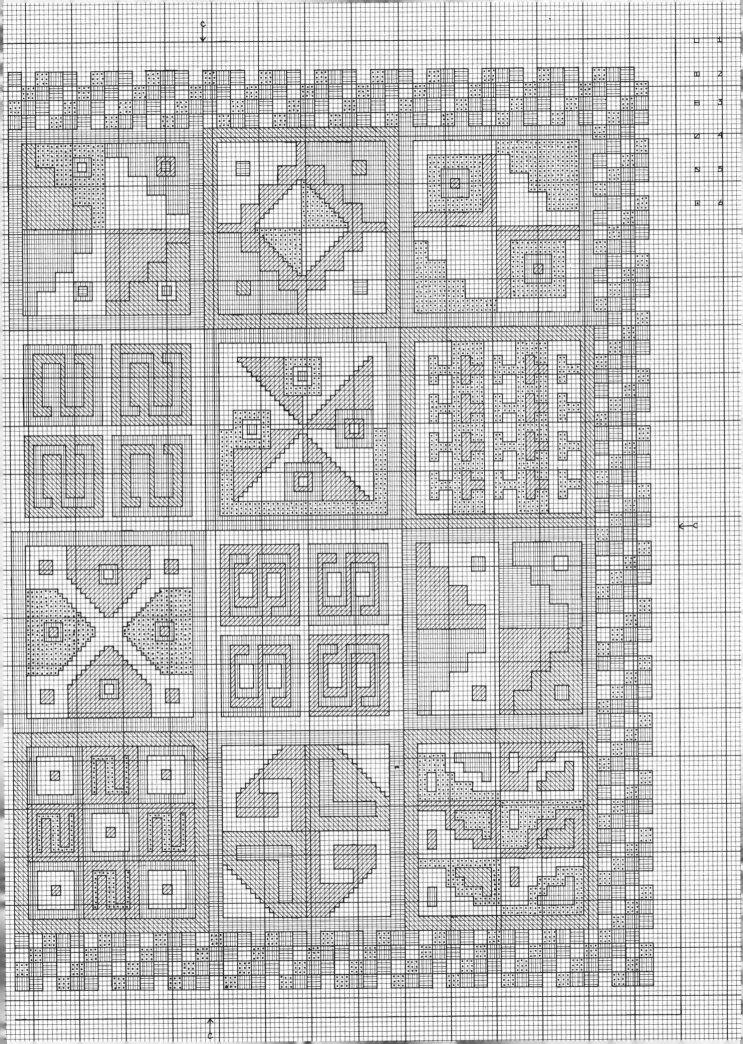

15. Peruvian Wall Hanging

14 1/2″ × 18 1/2″—Color Plate Page 72

This piece was derived from a small, narrow band of weaving in the collection of the Metropolitan Museum of Art, New York (Peruvian highlands, Tiahuanacan II culture, early ninth century, pre-Inca period). The coloring of the original textile is preserved as nearly as possible in this design, although it's difficult to tell to what extent time has altered the colors as they were when first hand-spun and dyed with plant materials.

CANVAS: 10 mesh to the inch. Design covers 143 mesh horizontally by 183 mesh vertically; a piece of canvas at least 16 1/2″ by 20 1/2″ will be sufficient.

NEEDLE: #18

YARNS: Use the full strand of Persian yarn in the following amounts:
1) white, 25 yds.
2) light seafoam green, 18 yds.
3) medium taupe, 43 yds.
4) brick red, 130 yds.
5) black, 48 yds.

STITCH: Basketweave

NOTE: In the graph, the tenth rectangle from the right across the top is to be 7 stitches wide instead of 6, and across the bottom, the eleventh rectangle from the right is also to be 7 instead of 6.

27

44

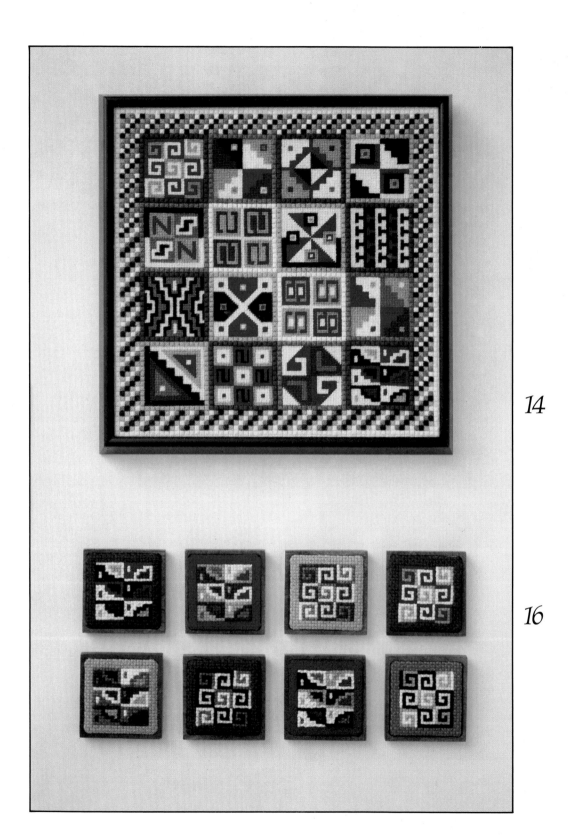

14

16

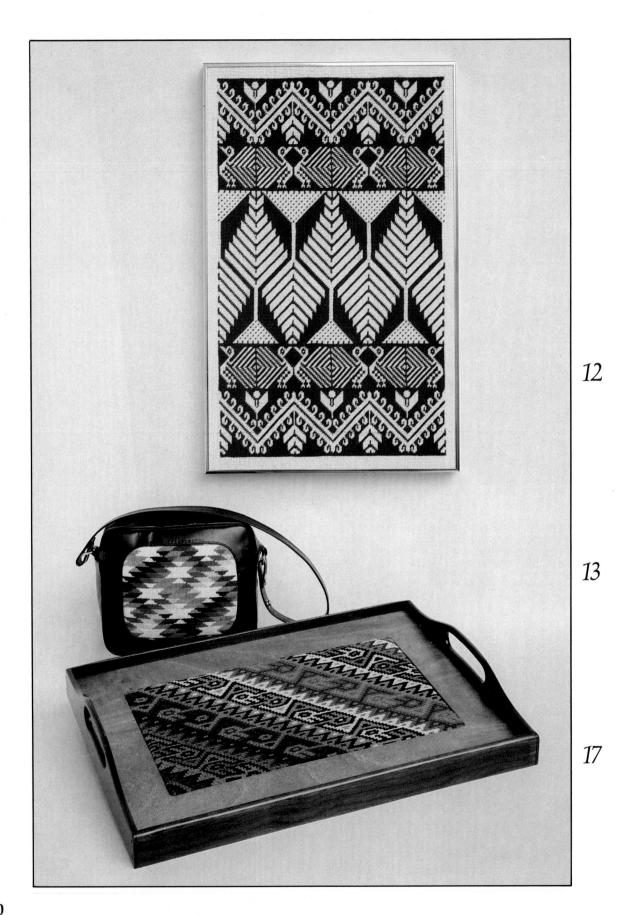

12

13

17

6

7

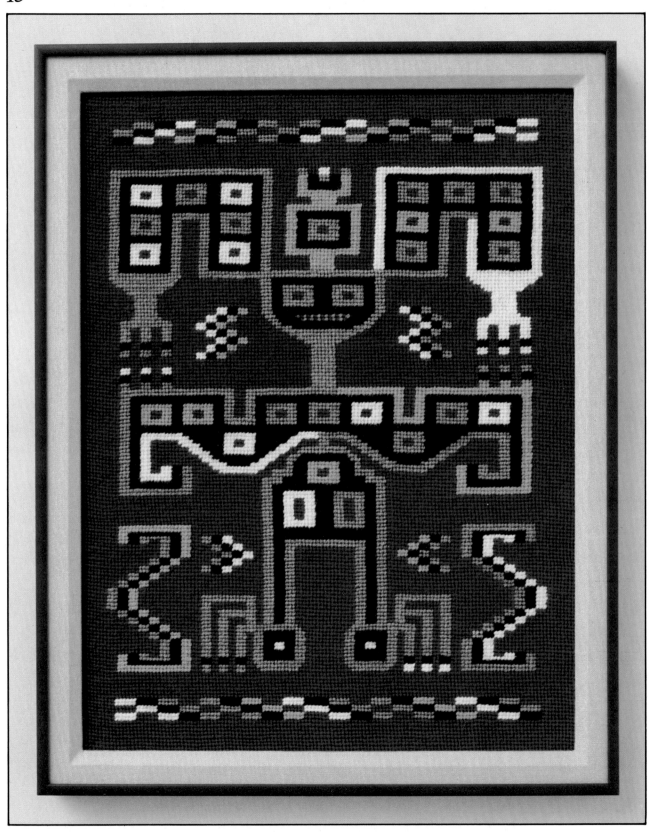

16. Inca Poncho Motif, Coasters

3 1/2″ × 3 1/2″—COLOR PLATE PAGE 69

To work these coasters, follow the graph for the upper-left- and the lower-right-square motifs of the Inca poncho wall hanging on pages 62–63, considering them Coaster A and Coaster B. Three alternate color arrangements for each design are given below. You may use any of the other square motifs, but I chose these as the pattern of each was amenable to being worked with the Mosaic stitch, alternating, thus requiring no blocking. Worked according to the following specifications, the designs will fit exactly into wooden, cork-backed frames made by Sudberry House (see SOURCES).

Use 14-mesh-to-the-inch canvas with #20 or #22 needle. You may work all of the designs on one piece of canvas, spacing them at least an inch and a half apart, or, work them on small leftover pieces of canvas which you can more easily carry with you. The border around each design should be 3 rows of Mosaic stitch, alternating, covering 6 rows of canvas mesh, rather than one row of Scotch stitch, alternating, covering 3 rows of canvas mesh, as in the poncho graph.

The following are three alternate color arrangements for each coaster pattern, plus yarn amounts for each design. In each case, substitute the color beside each number as it appears in the graph for the color under each alternate coaster design. Freely choose colors which suit you better, if you wish, but assign them numbers, as in this plan, to keep them well distributed among the whole set of coasters.

COASTER A	COASTER A1	COASTER A2	COASTER A3
1) white, 4 yds.	white	coral	gold
2) medium gold, 1 yd.	coral	black	coral
4) bright red, 2 yds.	gold	white	white
5) deep bright blue, 9 yds.	red	gold	red
6) black, 3 yds.	black	blue	blue

COASTER B	COASTER B1	COASTER B2	COASTER B3
1) white, 5 yds.	white	white	white
2) medium gold, 4 yds.	coral	gold	coral
4) bright red, 4 yds.	blue	black	black
5) deep bright blue, 8 yds.	gold	coral	blue

NOTE: See accompanying photo illustrating the simple procedure for mounting each coaster onto the cardboard square that is included with each coaster frame. After mounting each design, you can lightly brush rubber cement onto the back of the cardboard and onto the cutout area of the coaster frame; allow this to dry for a few minutes, then press the design into the frame.

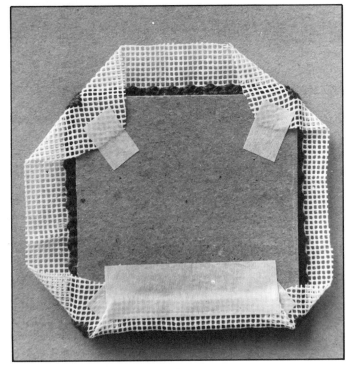

17. Peruvian Design, Tray

18″ × 10″—Color Plate Page 70

This repeated bird-motif pattern was adapted from a woolen tapestry-woven blanket of the late Ica period, pre-Conquest, found in Nazca. Almost ever-present elements in Peruvian decorative arts are the geometrical designs that owe their origins to the technique of basketry. The colors here are my own arrangement of the kind of earthy tones often found in this type of weaving.

CANVAS: 14 mesh to the inch. Design covers 244 mesh horizontally by 138 mesh vertically; a piece of canvas at least 20″ by 12″ will be sufficient.

NEEDLE: #22

YARNS: Separate Persian yarn and use two threads; you will need the following amounts before separating:
1) bright rust (medium terracotta), 24 yds.
2) light terracotta, 27 yds.
3) light gold, 30 yds.
4) dark gold, 30 yds.
5) black, 43 yds.
6) white, 27 yds.

STITCH: Mosaic, alternating

NOTE: The design was worked to fit the cutout area of a wooden tray, which comes with glass top, made by Sudberry House (see SOURCES).

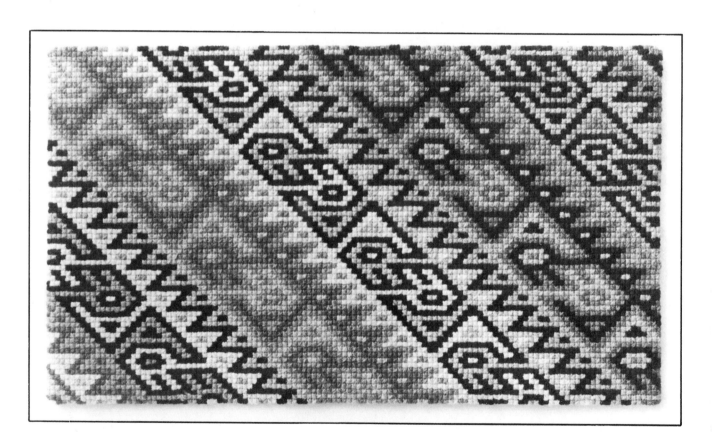

European Designs

18. Welsh Design, Red Cushion

10 1/4″ × 10 1/4″—Color Plate Page 91

From a traditional Welsh woolen cloth comes the pattern for this piece, and for the following two, as well.

CANVAS: 13 mesh to the inch. Design covers a 132-mesh square; a square of canvas at least 12 1/4″ by 12 1/4″ will be sufficient.

NEEDLE: #20 or #22

YARNS: Separate Persian yarn and use two threads; you will need the following amounts before separating:

1) Kelly green, 18 yds.
2) violet, 18 yds.
3) dark red, 95 yds.

STITCH: Mosaic, alternating

19. Welsh Design, Black Cushion

14" × 14"—Color Plate Page 91

This design utilizes the same basic pattern as the previous red cushion. However, in this instance, the center falls on the "circular" element of the pattern, rather than on the "cross."

CANVAS: 14 mesh to the inch. Design covers a 196-mesh square; a square of canvas at least 16" by 16" will be sufficient.
NEEDLE: #22
YARNS: Separate Persian yarn and use two threads; you will need the following amounts before separating:
  1) Kelly green, 35 yds.
  2) deep bright blue, 35 yds.
  3) black, 130 yds.
  STITCH: Mosaic, alternating

20. Welsh Design Portfolio

The basic Welsh pattern is again utilized here for the canvas insert of a tan leather portfolio from Toni Totes of Vermont (see Sources).

CANVAS: 12 mesh to the inch. Design covers 180 mesh horizontally by 92 mesh vertically.
NEEDLE: #20 or #22
YARNS: Separate Persian yarn and use two threads; you will need the following amounts before separating:
  1) light seafoam green, 15 yds.
  2) deep seafoam green, 15 yds.
  3) medium rust, 80 yds.
  STITCH: Mosaic, alternating

Note: Center pattern on the "cross" motif of the graphed design.

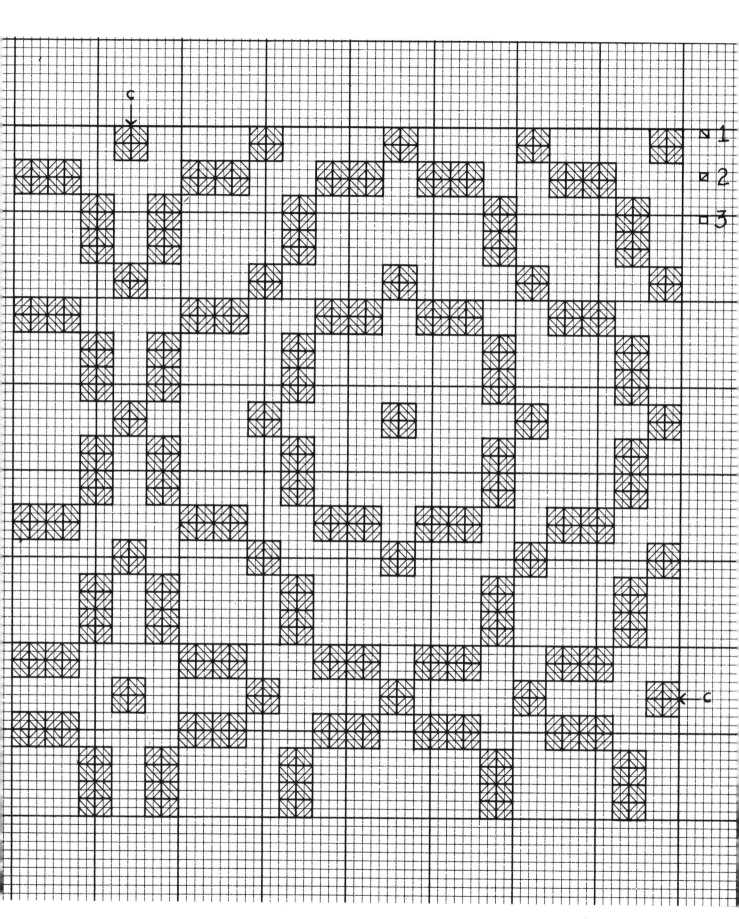

21. Macqueen Tartan Cushion

14 1/2″ × 14 1/2″—Color Plate Page 91

This and the following two designs are careful adaptations of authentic Scottish clan tartans. In this case, and that of the Davidson tartan cushion, the basic stitch forming the diagonal lines of the design simulates the "twill" effect of the original woven textiles.

CANVAS: 14 mesh to the inch. Design covers a 204-mesh square; a square of canvas at least 16 1/2″ by 16 1/2″ will be sufficient.

NEEDLE: #22

YARNS: Separate Persian yarn and use two threads; you will need the following amounts before separating:

1) lemon yellow, 5 yds.
2) bright red, 125 yds.
3) black, 85 yds.

STITCH: Basketweave

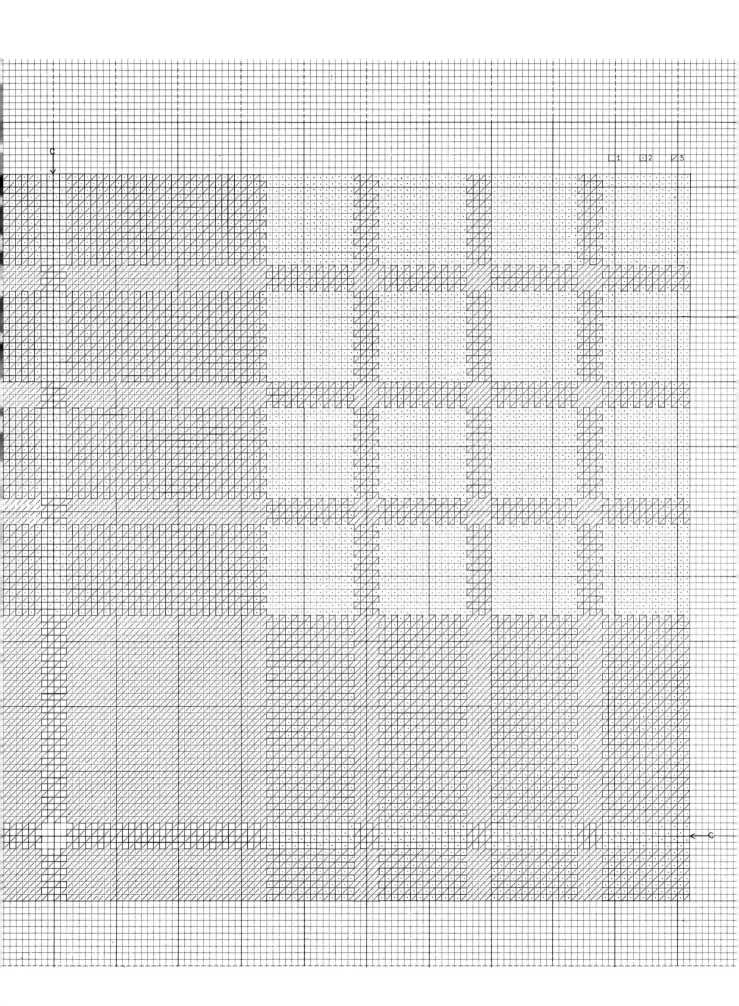

22. Davidson Tartan Cushion

12″ × 12″—Color Plate Page 91

CANVAS: 14 mesh to the inch. Design covers a 166-mesh square; a square of canvas at least 14″ by 14″ will be sufficient.

NEEDLE: #22

YARNS: Separate Persian yarn and use two threads; you will need the following amounts before separating:

1) bright green, 40 yds.
2) bright red, 10 yds.
3) deep bright blue, 24 yds.
4) black, 30 yds.

STITCH: Basketweave

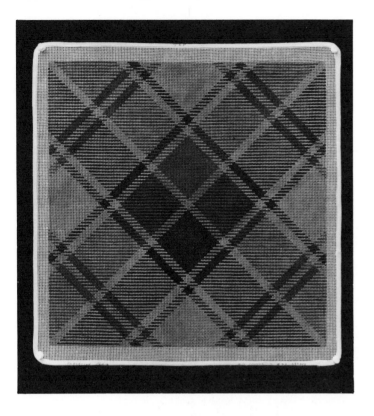

23. Robertson Tartan, Painted Canvas

13" × 13"

Another authentic tartan, set "on the bias" in this instance, provides the design for this piece and for the following tennis-racket cover. Here the twill effect is achieved by the horizontal stripes.

CANVAS: 14 mesh to the inch. Design covers a 183-mesh square; a square of canvas 15" by 15" will be sufficient.

NEEDLE: #22

YARNS: Separate Persian yarn and use two threads; you will need the following amounts before separating:

1) bright lime green, 32 yds.
2) deep bright blue, 32 yds.
3) bright red, 60 yds.

STITCH: Continental (stripes), Basketweave (large areas)

24. Robertson Tartan, Tennis-Racket Cover

COLOR PLATE PAGE 91

CANVAS: This design was worked on the 10-mesh-to-the-inch canvas insert of a prefinished tennis-racket cover made by Needlepoint, U.S.A. (see SOURCES).

NEEDLE: #18

YARNS: Use the full strand of Persian yarn in the following amounts:

1) bright lime green, 28 yds.
2) deep bright blue, 28 yds.
3) bright red, 55 yds.

STITCH: Continental (stripes), Basketweave (large areas)

NOTE: To work the design, use the graph for the preceding design; find the center of the canvas insert and follow the graph, starting at the center, marked *o*, and working out to the edges of the tennis-racket cover.

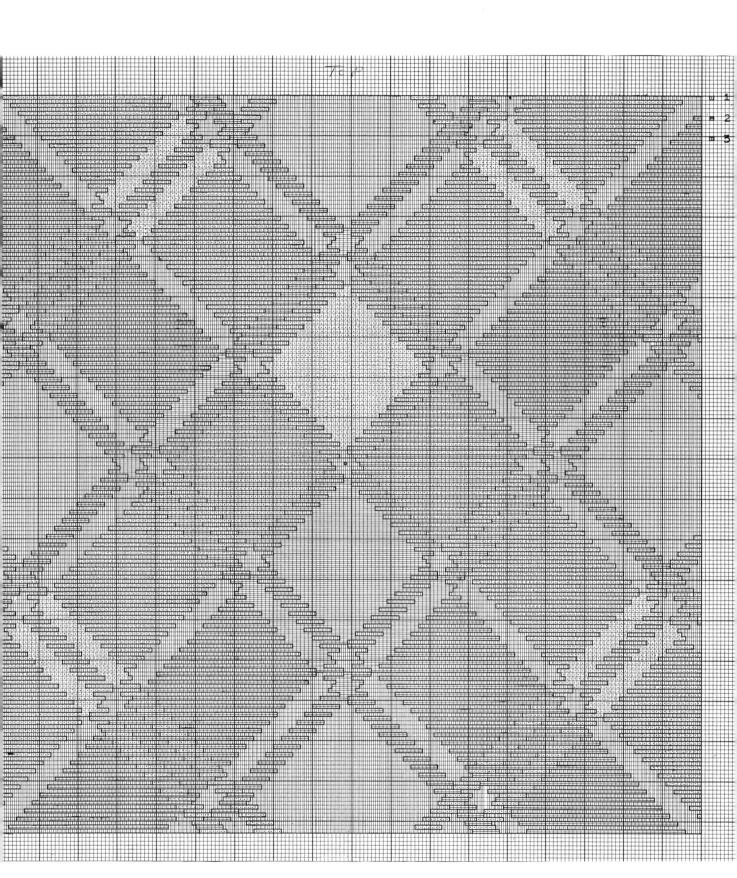

1
2
3

25. French Cushion

17″ × 11 1/4″—Color Plate Page 94

From an early-nineteenth-century French textile, Empire style, in the collection of the Cooper-Hewitt Museum, New York, come the design and colors for this piece.

CANVAS: 14 mesh to the inch. Design covers 239 mesh horizontally by 157 mesh vertically; a piece of canvas at least 19″ by 13 1/4″ will be sufficient. If you use a prefinished cushion with canvas insert made by Alice Peterson Company (see SOURCES), as we did, the mesh count will probably differ slightly. Therefore, you will have to find the center mesh of the canvas insert and begin there, following the graph from the center of the design. You may have less room at the top and bottom of the canvas; if so, you may adjust the number of stitches in the horizontal end bands.

NEEDLE: #22

YARNS: Separate Persian yarn and use two threads; you will need the following amounts before separating:
1) white, 50 yds.
2) light terracotta, 6 yds.
3) rust, 35 yds.
4) light taupe, 28 yds.
5) brown, 17 yds.
6) black, 30 yds.
STITCH: Basketweave

NOTE: Asterisk serves as a reminder that the area between these two rosettes spans nine horizontal canvas mesh, rather than ten; repeat this change as you work the other half of the design.

34

37

62

57, 58

29

19

18

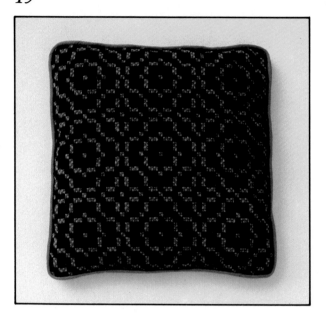

21

22

24

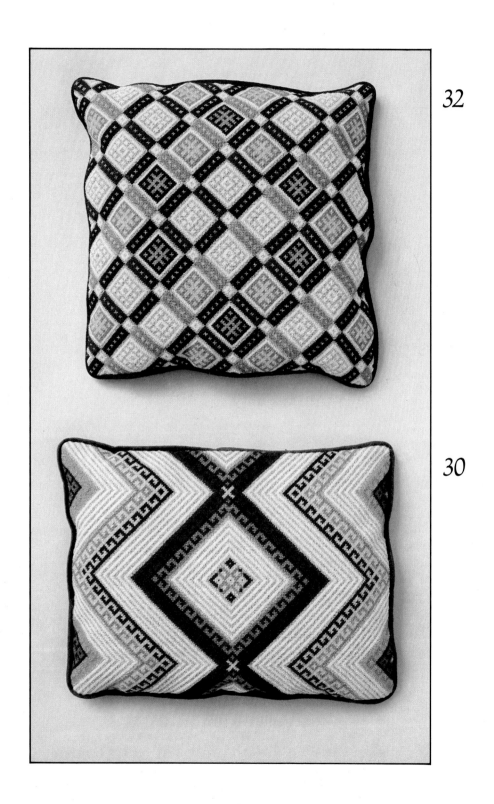

43

32

30

26

25

38

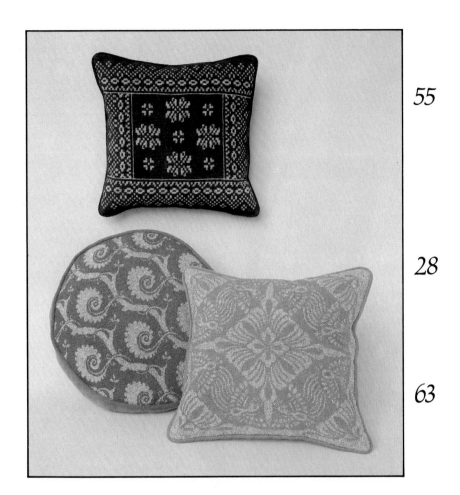

55

28

63

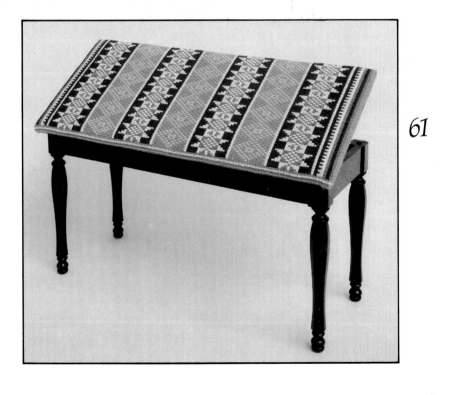

61

26. German Cushion

13 1/2" × 13 1/2"—Color Plate Page 94

A thirteenth-century Regensburg German textile inspired this design. I chose a deep brown for the ground color, but any deep tone would be handsome.

CANVAS: 12 mesh to the inch. Design, as graphed, covers a 162-mesh square. If you wish to work the design round, as in the picture, use perfectly square canvas (see Sources); find the center of your canvas *between* horizontal and vertical rows of mesh and count 81 mesh in each direction toward the edges. Mark the space after the eighty-first mesh. Place the point of a compass in the center hole and extend the radius to one of the outer marks. Draw a circle onto the canvas. This design was worked on the canvas insert of a round prefinished cushion-cover from Alice Peterson Company (see Sources) which comes with its own inner cushion and zips open around its boxed edge. In this instance, the center was located as above and the design was worked out to the edges, extending the pattern an extra row or two of mesh as necessary.

NEEDLE: #20 or #22

YARNS: Separate Persian yarn and use two threads; you will need the following amounts before separating:

1) white, 50 yds.
2) deep brown, 90 yds.

STITCH: Mosaic, alternating

99

27. Spanish Cushion

16 1/2" × 16"—COLOR PLATE PAGE 65

The pattern for this piece was adapted from one of the bands of a woven silk sash of the type known as "Hispano-Moresque," in the collection of the Textile Museum, Washington, D.C. (Granada, *ca.* 1400). This represents an example of the geometric device of *laceria*, resembling interlaced canework, typical of the period. I chose colors characteristic of this phase of Spanish weaving.

CANVAS: 10 mesh to the inch. Design covers 165 mesh horizontally by 159 mesh vertically; a piece of canvas at least 18 1/2" by 18" will be sufficient.

NEEDLE: #18

YARNS: Use the full strand of Persian yarn in the following amounts:

1) medium gold, 130 yds.
2) yellow-orange, 10 yds.
3) coral pink, 12 yds.
4) medium gray, 70 yds.
5) violet, 50 yds.
6) powder blue, 28 yds.

STITCH: Basketweave

28. Venetian Cushion

17" diameter—COLOR PLATE PAGE 95

The design for this piece comes from a fifteenth-century Italian brocade in the type of intertwining, stylized floral pattern popular during the period. I've chosen to work it with olive green and metallic gold, but it would be equally handsome worked with burgundy or Delft blue as the background color.

CANVAS: 13 mesh to the inch. Design covers a 222-mesh-diameter circle; a square of canvas at least 19" by 19" will be sufficient.

NEEDLE: #20

YARNS: Separate Persian yarn and use two threads; you will need the following amount before separating:

1) olive green, 120 yds.

Bucilla Spotlight, using a single strand:

2) gold, 1 1/2 spools

STITCH: Basketweave

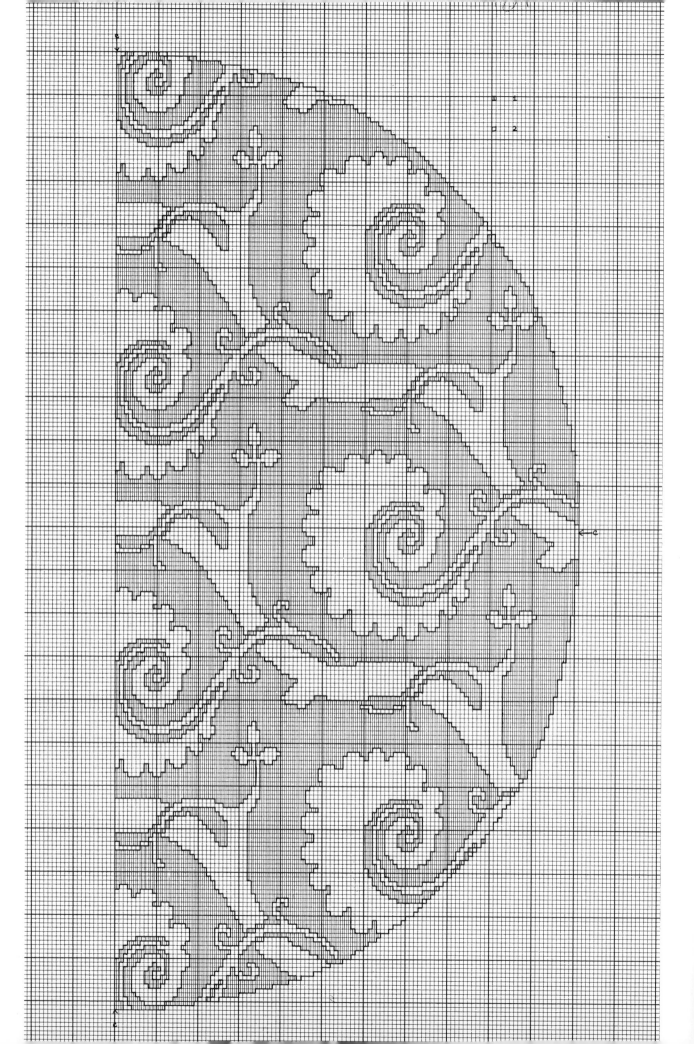

29. Swedish Tea Cozy

15″ × 10 1/2″—COLOR PLATE PAGE 90

The motifs in this design come from several Swedish woven textiles, most notably from a wall hanging in the collection of the Brooklyn Museum. Swedish tradition and a bright, sunny kitchen suggested the coloring for the piece, but the design is amenable to a number of combinations, for instance, earth tones, preserving the yellow and orange of the design, but substituting deep brown and rust for the blues.

CANVAS: 14 mesh to the inch. Design covers 210 mesh horizontally across the bottom edge by 146 mesh vertically at highest edge; a piece of canvas at least 17″ by 12 1/2″ will be sufficient.
NEEDLE: #22

YARNS: Separate Persian yarn and use two threads; you will need the following amounts before separating:
1) white, 25 yds.
2) bright yellow, 25 yds.
3) bright orange, 15 yds.
4) medium sky blue, 75 yds.
5) deep bright blue, 50 yds.
STITCH: Mosaic, alternating

NOTE: The graph for this design is reproduced upside down in order that you may begin to work along the straight edges and establish the pattern before working in along the curved edges. After working the dark-blue border, you'll find it easy to fill in the medium-blue background areas if you work the inner design motifs first. We found that quilted corduroy made a very nice backing material; it worked well for the corded edge, too. As it is self-backed, no lining is necessary.

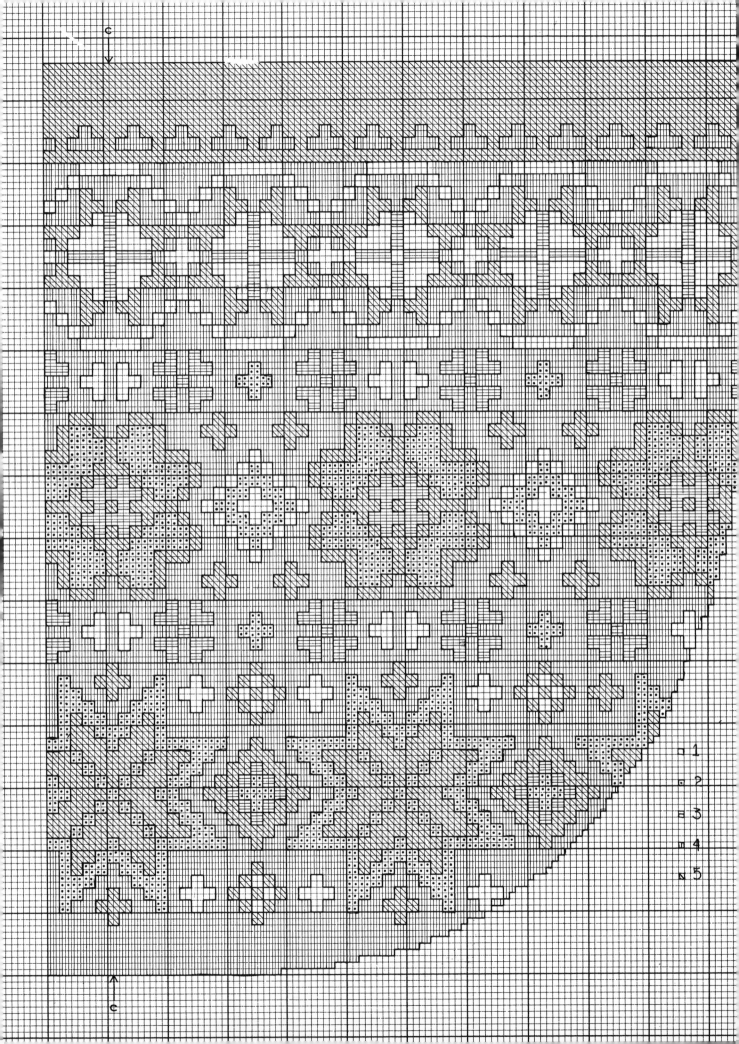

30. *Bulgarian Cushion, Central Diamond Motif*

17 1/2" × 13 1/2"—Color Plate Page 93

A beautiful Balkan textile in the collection of the Metropolitan Museum inspired this design. The colors, including the metallic gold, closely approximate those of the original.

CANVAS: 14 mesh to the inch. Design covers 241 mesh horizontally by 187 mesh vertically; a piece of canvas at least 19 1/2" by 15 1/2" will be sufficient.

NEEDLE: #20

YARNS: Separate Persian yarn and use two threads; you will need the following amounts before separating:

1) white, 80 yds.
2) lemon yellow, 22 yds.
3) lilac, 30 yds.
4) bright red, 33 yds.
5) deep bright blue, 13 yds.
6) medium bright green, 8 yds.
7) deep bright green, 13 yds.

Bucilla Spotlight, using a single strand:

8) gold, 1 spool

STITCH: Basketweave

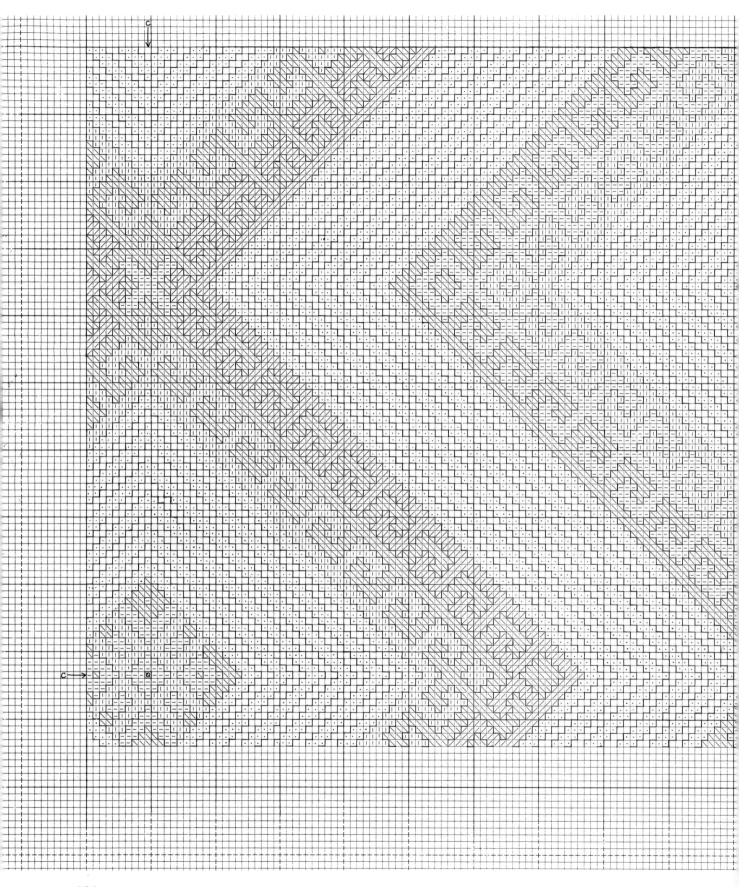

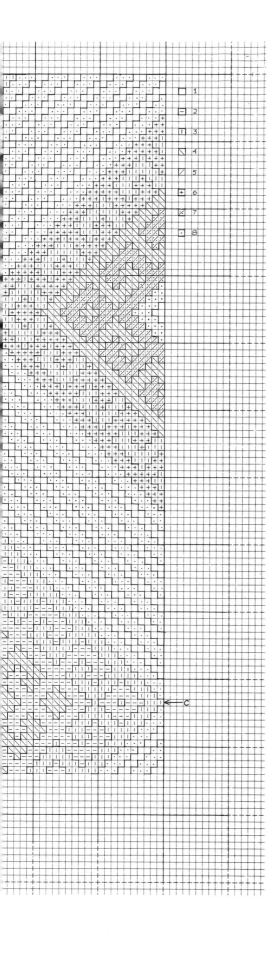

31. Bulgarian Design, Central Diamond Motif, Glasses Case

This piece was worked using a prefinished glasses case from Alice Peterson Company (see SOURCES). To create the pattern, I took an interesting section of the graph for the preceding cushion, along the top edge toward the center, and extended the pattern to bring it out to the edge of the glasses case.

CANVAS: The prefinished case is composed of two pieces of 14-mesh-to-the-inch canvas joined together with a zipper (in this case, red) which, when opened up, allows each piece of canvas to flatten out so that you can work the needlepoint easily.

NEEDLE: #20

YARNS: Separate Persian yarn and use two threads; you will need the following amounts before separating:

1) white, 10 yds.
2) lemon yellow, 5 yds.
3) lilac, 8 yds.
4) bright red, 10 yds.
5) deep bright blue, 4 yds.

Bucilla Spotlight, using a single strand:

8) gold, 20 yds.

STITCH: Basketweave

NOTE: You may finish the edges with an edging stitch, if you like (see SOURCES), and line the inside of the case with a complementary lightweight fabric, such as cotton.

32. Bulgarian Cushion, Overall Diamond Motif

16″ × 16″—COLOR PLATE PAGE 93

Another textile from the Metropolitan Museum's collection provides the design for this piece (see frontispiece).

CANVAS: 14 mesh to the inch. Design covers a 223-mesh square; a square of canvas at least 18″ by 18″ will be sufficient.
NEEDLE: #20
YARNS: Separate Persian yarn and use two threads; you will need the following amounts before separating:
1) white, 45 yds.
2) lemon yellow, 16 yds.
3) lilac, 40 yds.
4) bright red, 55 yds.
5) deep bright blue, 30 yds.
6) medium bright green, 10 yds.
Bucilla Spotlight, using a single strand:
7) silver, 1 1/2 spools
STITCH: Basketweave

33. Bulgarian Design, Overall Diamond Motif, Glasses Case

This piece was worked using a prefinished glasses case from Alice Peterson Company (see SOURCES). To work this design using the graph for the preceding cushion, turn the prefinished case (with navy zipper) upside down; find the center mesh stitch, match this with the center grid square on the graph, and follow the pattern, working out to the edges of the case. See the directions for the Bulgarian glasses case, central diamond motif (31), for notes on working and finishing the case.

NEEDLE: #20
YARNS: Separate Persian yarn and use two threads; you will need the following amounts before separating:
1) white, 10 yds.
2) lemon yellow, 1 yd.
3) lilac, 3 yds.
4) bright red, 4 yds.
5) deep bright blue, 2 yds.
Bucilla Spotlight, using a single strand:
7) silver, 25 yds.
STITCH: Basketweave

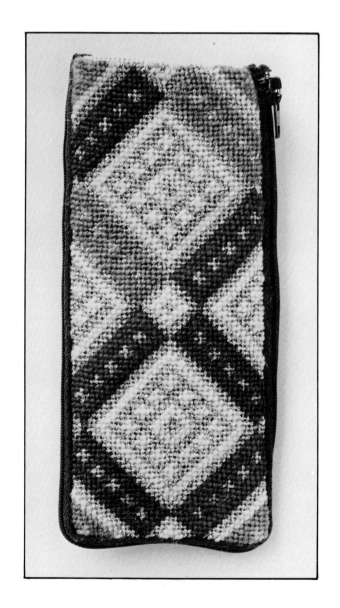

110

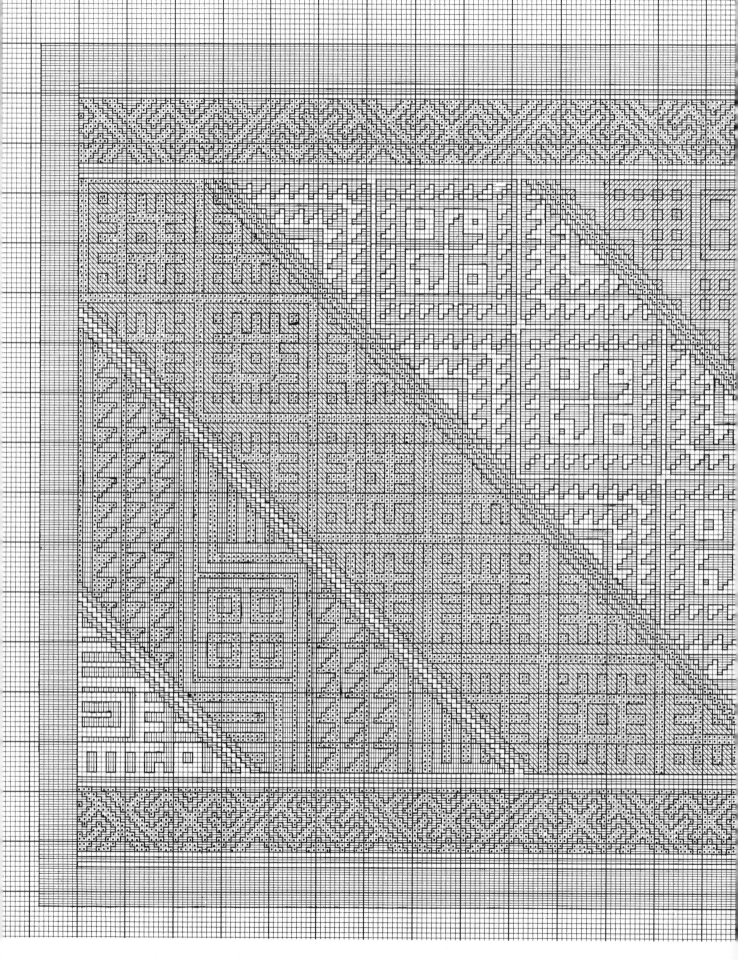

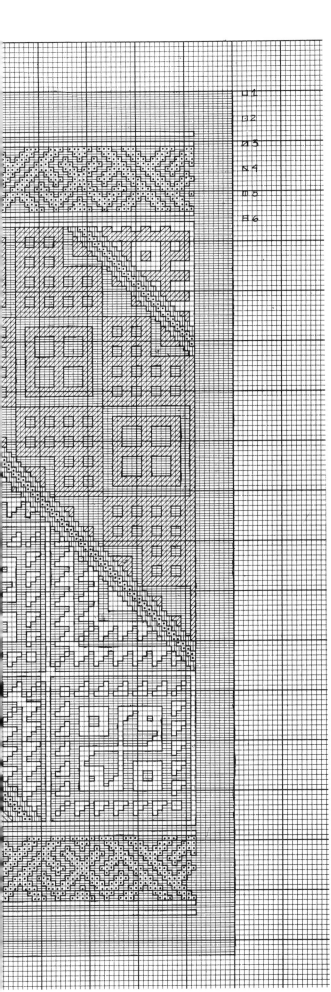

34. Lithuanian Design I, Cushion

16 1/2″ × 14 1/2″—COLOR PLATE PAGE 89

Clear, vibrant colors characterize Lithuanian woven sashes, several of which I have used here to form the diagonal elements of this design, as well as the upper and lower bands.

CANVAS: 12 mesh to the inch. Design covers 198 mesh horizontally by 173 mesh vertically; a piece of canvas at least 18 1/2″ by 16 1/2″ will be sufficient.

NEEDLE: #20 or #22

YARNS: Separate Persian yarn and use two threads; you will need the following amounts before separating:

1) lemon yellow, 36 yds.
2) hot pink, 40 yds.
3) yellow-orange, 13 yds.
4) red-orange, 18 yds.
5) medium violet, 24 yds.
6) bright green, 36 yds.

STITCH: Basketweave

35. Lithuanian Design I, Christmas Stocking

The previous design was used to work the canvas insert of a prefinished, zippered, red canvas Christmas stocking made by Needlepoint, U.S.A. (see Sources).

CANVAS: 12 mesh to the inch
NEEDLE: #20 or #22
YARNS: Separate Persian yarn and use two threads; you will need the following amounts before separating:

1) lemon yellow, 14 yds.
2) hot pink, 13 yds.
3) yellow-orange, 8 yds.
4) bright red (instead of red-orange), 10 yds.
5) medium violet, 7 yds.
6) bright green, 20 yds.
STITCH: Scotch, alternating

NOTE: Work your first Scotch stitch in the upper right-hand corner of the design (in first white stripe of border) so that its diagonals point to that corner. In this manner, the alternating halves of the Scotch stitches will fall along the stripes, creating smooth diagonal lines.

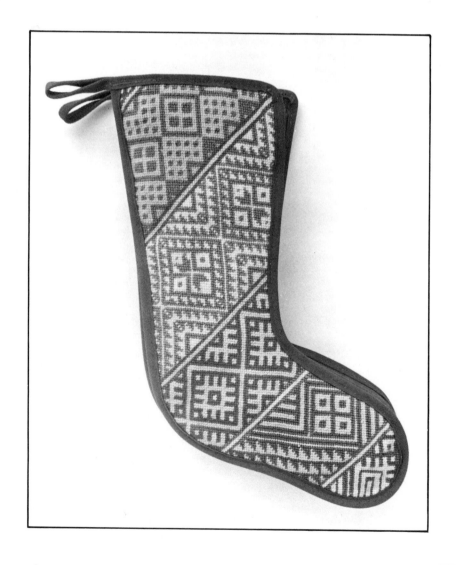

36. Lithuanian Design II, Painted Canvas

13 1/2″ × 13 1/2″

This design represents another use of Lithuanian sash strips, which are placed on the diagonal to form an interesting design. In this case, every element of the design covers the appropriate number of mesh to make it workable in the Scotch stitch, alternating; the following Granny bag design, which is adapted from this design, illustrates the use of the Scotch stitch.

CANVAS: 14 mesh to the inch. Design covers a 189-mesh square; a piece of canvas at least 15 1/2″ by 15 1/2″ will be sufficient.

NEEDLE: #22

YARNS: Separate Persian yarn and use two threads; you will need the following amounts before separating:

1) white, 40 yds.
2) lemon yellow, 18 yds.
3) hot pink, 14 yds.
4) bright orange, 10 yds.
5) bright red, 10 yds.
6) violet, 17 yds.
7) sky blue, 30 yds.
8) bright green, 3 yds.

STITCH: Scotch, alternating

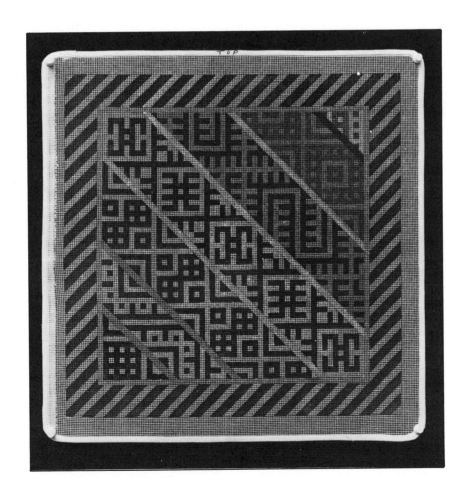

37. Lithuanian Design II, Granny Bag

COLOR PLATE PAGE 89

The canvas insert of a blue denim Granny bag from Needlepoint, U.S.A. (see SOURCES) was worked using the graph of the previous design.

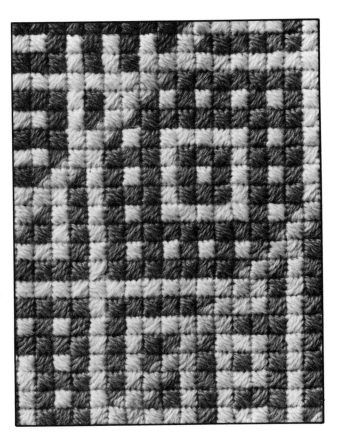

CANVAS: 10 mesh to the inch
NEEDLE: #18
YARNS: Use the full strand of Persian yarn in the following amounts:
1) white, 24 yds.
2) lemon yellow, 21 yds.
3) hot pink, 10 yds.
6) violet, 17 yds.
7) sky blue, 26 yds.
8) bright green, 6 yds.
STITCH: Scotch, alternating

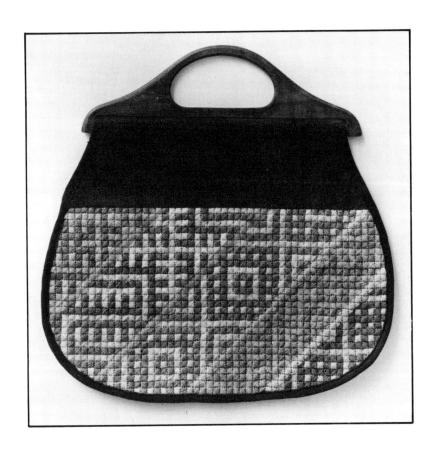

38. Latvian Cushion

14 1/2″ × 10″—COLOR PLATE PAGE 94

This design is composed of horizontal bands derived from several traditional Latvian woven sash patterns. Hot, brilliant colors are more typical of these, but I chose earthy tones instead for this piece.

CANVAS: 10 mesh to the inch. Design covers 145 mesh horizontally by 99 mesh vertically; a piece of canvas at least 16 1/2″ by 12″ will be sufficient.

NEEDLE: #18

YARNS: Use the full strand of Persian yarn in the following amounts:

1) white, 100 yds.
2) medium gold, 9 yds.
3) rust, 55 yds.
4) black, 50 yds.

STITCH: Basketweave

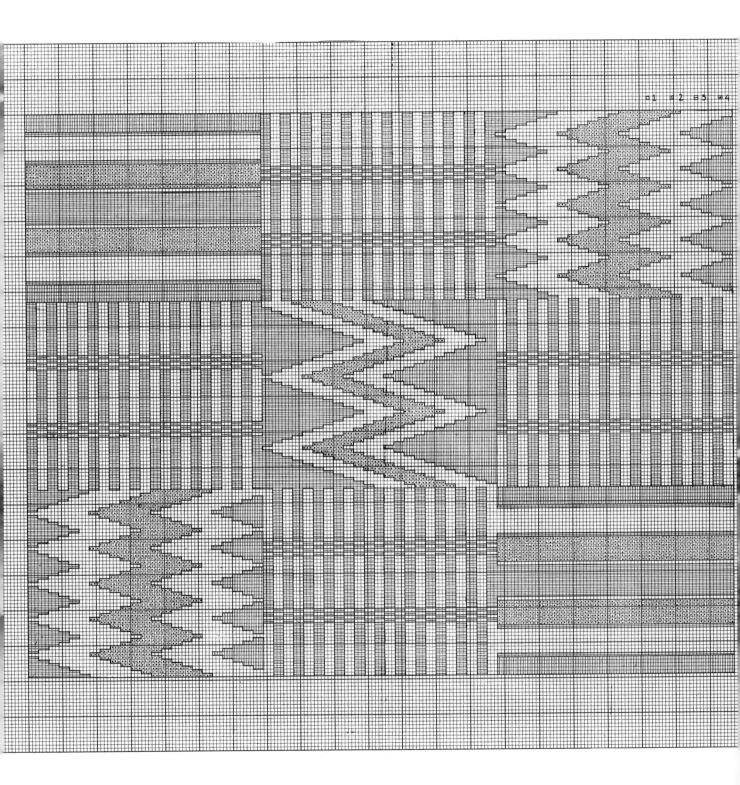

African Designs

39. Ashanti Kente-Cloth Cushion

16″ × 12 1/4″—Color Plate Page 134

The design of this piece combines elements of several examples of the textiles hand-woven by men in Ghana, especially at Bonwire. A large piece of cloth is made by first weaving a very long, narrow strip, which is then cut into shorter lengths and sewn together. In order to achieve the kind of well-organized and harmonious design typical of these cloths, a good deal of complicated planning ahead must take place in the process of weaving the original narrow strip. These cloths are used as mantles, wraparounds, and blankets. The colors used for this design are those one might find in an example of this cloth, and the straight Gobelin stitch effectively simulates the "raised" character of weft threads covering warp threads.

CANVAS: 13 mesh to the inch. Design spans 207 *holes* horizontally by 159 *holes* vertically; a piece of canvas at least 18″ by 14 1/4″ will be sufficient.

NEEDLE: #20

YARNS: Use the full strand of Persian yarn in the following amounts:
  1) bright golden yellow, 70 yds.
  2) bright red, 50 yds.
  3) jade green, 15 yds.
  4) black, 25 yds.

STITCH: Straight Gobelin, 4 holes high (see stitch diagram).

NOTE: See page 19, FOLLOWING THE GRAPHS, for explanation of how to follow this particular graph.

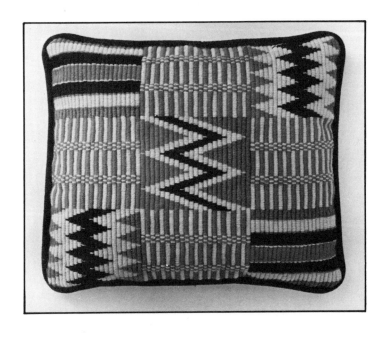

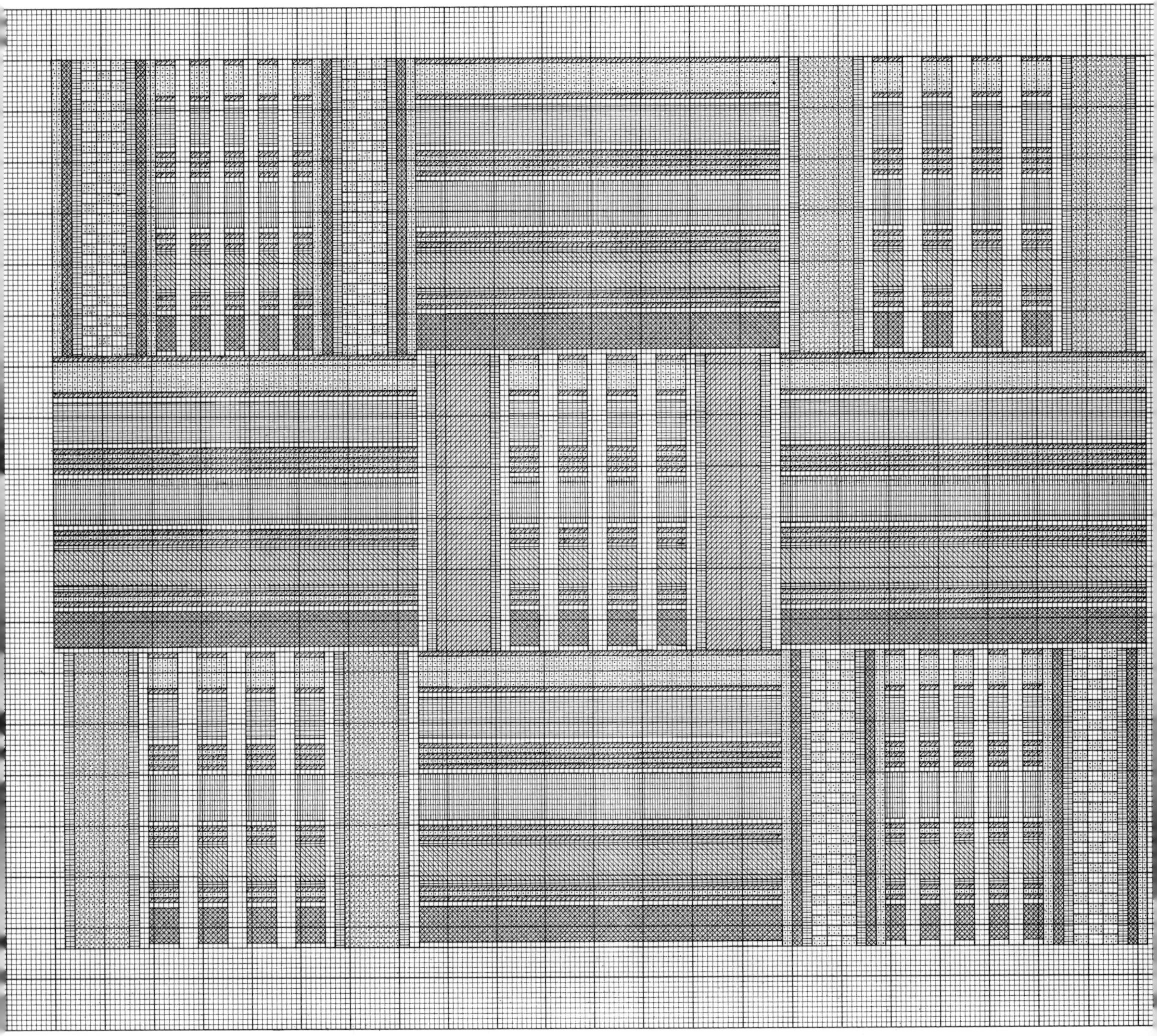

40. West African Men's-Weave Design, Cushion

16 1/4" × 12 1/2"—Color Plates Pages 134, 135

An incredibly beautiful cloth, also woven by men in Ghana, inspired the design for this piece. I saw the original textile at the exhibition of *African Textiles and Decorative Arts* held in 1972 at the Museum of Modern Art in New York. The original cloth closely resembles the *kente* cloth, but the brilliance of the colors and the asymmetry of the stripes are quite unusual.

CANVAS: 14 mesh to the inch. Design covers 222 mesh horizontally by 174 mesh vertically. A piece of canvas 18 1/4" by 14 1/2" will be sufficient.

NEEDLE: #22

YARNS: Separate Persian yarn and use two threads; you will need the following amounts before separating:
1) white, 30 yds.
2) maize yellow, 65 yds.
3) coral pink, 60 yds.
4) bright orange, 27 yds.
5) rose, 35 yds.
6) light lime green, 12 yds.
7) dark jade green, 50 yds.
8) blue-violet, 40 yds.
9) black, 40 yds.

STITCH: Knitting stitch, used both horizontally and vertically in the design.

Note: See page 19, under Following the Graphs, and also see the stitch diagram, page 28.

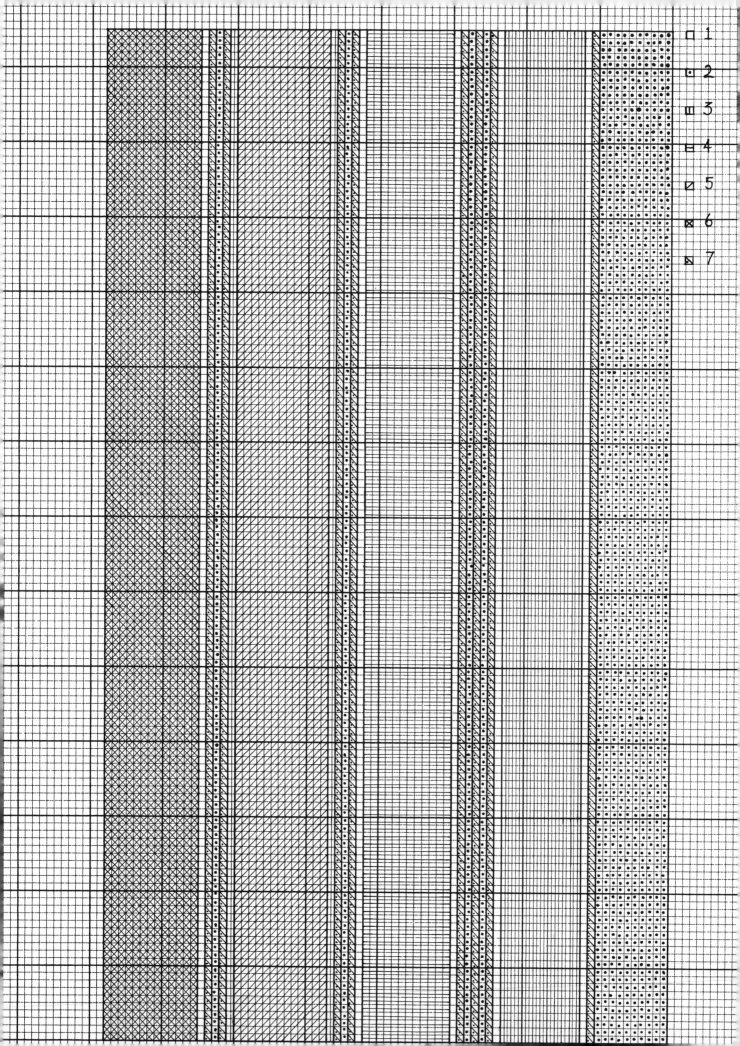

41. West African Men's-Weave Design, Stationery Box

10 1/2" × 6"

I found the colors and arrangement of the stripes in the preceding design so appealing that I decided to adapt them for this stationery box. The box, with a cutout area and a board for mounting the needlepoint canvas, comes from Needlepoint, U.S.A. (see Sources). I chose a blue box for this design, but it comes in several other colors. For the stitch, I chose to use the straight Gobelin, which simulates the effect of the weave.

CANVAS: 13 mesh to the inch. Design spans 136 *holes* horizontally by 78 *holes* vertically; a piece of canvas at least 12 1/2" by 8" will be sufficient.

NEEDLE: #20

YARNS: Use the full strand of Persian yarn in the following amounts:
1) white, 5 yds.
2) maize yellow, 10 yds.
3) coral pink, 9 yds.
4) rose, 8 yds.
5) dark jade green, 9 yds.
6) blue-violet, 9 yds.
7) black, 9 yds.

STITCH: Straight Gobelin, four holes high; each stitch lies adjacent to three vertical mesh of canvas. (See page 19, under Following the Graphs, and also page 29 for the stitch diagram.)

Note: See page 75, which illustrates mounting the work to a cardboard backing.

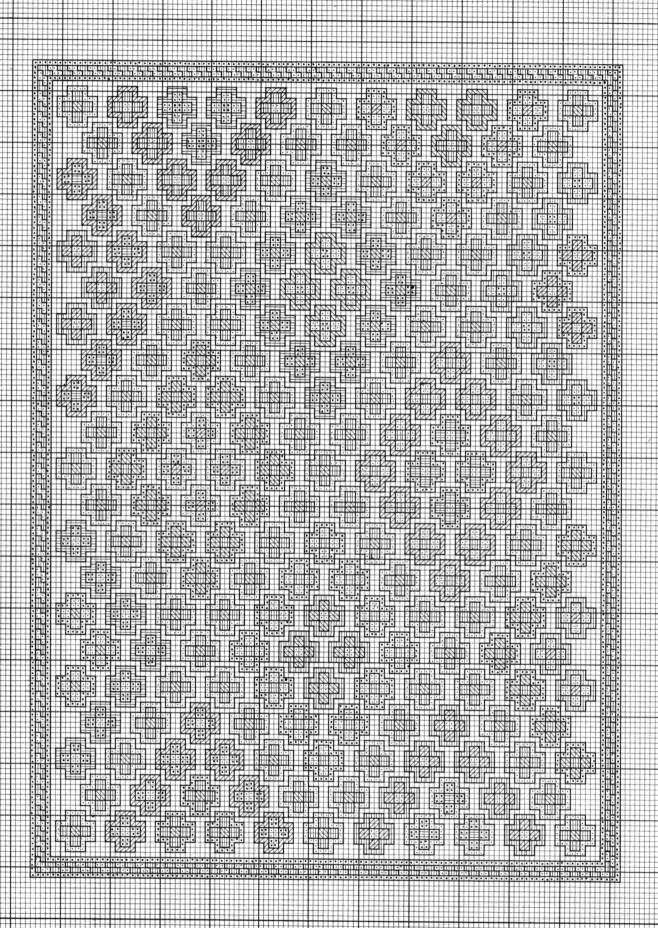

Middle Eastern Designs

42. Iranian Kirman Design, Painted Canvas

17 1/2″ × 13 1/2″

An unusual carpet of the Afshar type, woven in the Kirman region of Iran, lends its pattern to this design and to the upholstered chair on page 92. Its disarming simplicity makes it amenable to any number of color combinations, and because of its overall quality, the pattern may be repeated to be used for large objects and still retain its interest by "scattering" and recombining the colors for a random effect.

CANVAS: 10 mesh to the inch. Design covers 174 mesh horizontally by 134 mesh vertically. A piece of canvas at least 19 1/2″ by 15 1/2″ will be sufficient.

NEEDLE: #18

YARNS: Use the full strand of Persian yarn in the following amounts:
1) white, 60 yds.
2) light gold, 15 yds.
3) dark gold, 18 yds.
4) coral, 10 yds.
5) bright red, 30 yds.
6) deep Delft blue, 45 yds.
7) medium Delft blue, 70 yds.

STITCH: Basketweave

43. Iranian Kirman Design, Upholstered Chair

COLOR PLATE PAGE 92

After you have made a template of each area to be upholstered with the needlepoint design (see page 25, under FINISHING), fold each template exactly in half vertically; then go over your pencil outline of the shape on one side with a broad felt-tip marker, gently rounding the curved edges as you go. For each piece of canvas you will use, find the center mesh and lightly mark the horizontal and vertical rows of mesh that intersect at the center, using a fine permanent marker. Place the marked template under the canvas with the folded edge coinciding with the vertical center line on the canvas. (The dimension of your canvas should be at least 2" larger than the design overall.) Then trace the shape of the half-template onto the canvas with the fine marker. Turn the template over; you should be able to see the heavily marked shape through the paper. If it is rather indefinite, go over it again on this side. Then proceed to use this reversed shape to trace the other half of the template onto the canvas.

Follow the graph for the preceding Kirman design, beginning at the center and working out to the edges of your marked shape. Expand the pattern as follows:

Repeat the arrangement of colors with the diamond shapes defined by the diagonally-intersecting white-outlined crosses, taking care to avoid an alternating "every other" kind of look overall. The closest repeat of a particular arrangement should be, in chess terms, a "knight's move" away. Or, in other words, think of an L shape and repeat an arrangement two diamonds over diagonally and one diamond to the side, up or down. This will result in the "controlled randomness" so appealing to the eye and mind. For this pattern, it would be best to preserve the color arrangements within the diamonds as given, rather than recombine the colors in other possible arrangements, as these have been very carefully considered in terms of light and dark and relative brightness in order to achieve a balance within each diamond. If you decide to work the design in another group of colors altogether, be sure to substitute each color with another of similar value (lightness/darkness) and chroma (brightness: "warm," such as yellow or red, versus "cool," such as blue or green).

It would be very helpful to plan the entire piece in advance, working out the repeats. For notes on transferring the design from the graph to the canvas by means of paint or markers, see page 20, under FOLLOWING THE GRAPHS.

48

46

45

47

9

51

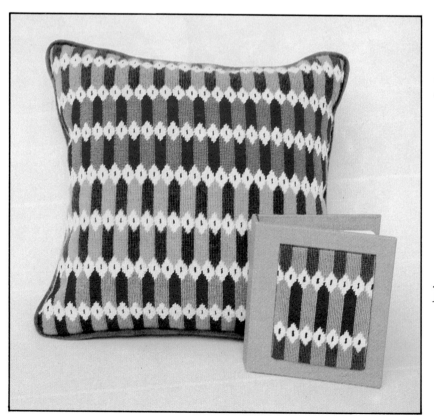

10

11

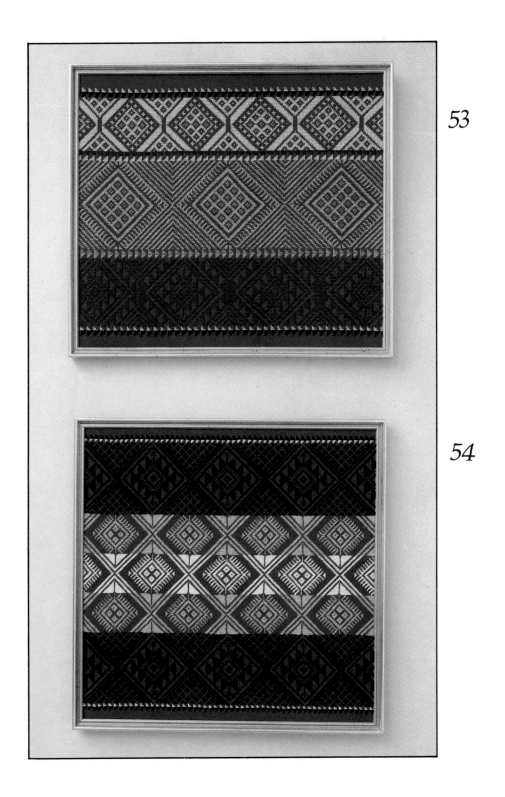

53

54

39

40

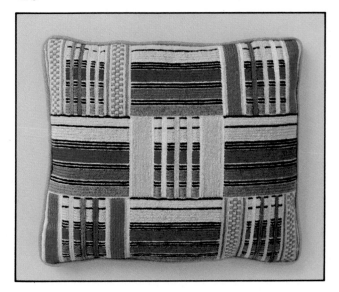

59

44. Armenian Cushion

16 1/2″ × 12 3/4″—COLOR PLATE PAGE 65

A carpet of the Sileh type from the Soviet Socialist Republic of Armenia contributed the motif for this design. In the original carpet, this motif is repeated ten times, in two rows of five each, to form a long, narrow piece.

CANVAS: 14 mesh to the inch. Design covers 232 mesh horizontally by 177 mesh vertically; a piece of canvas at least 18 1/2″ by 14 3/4″ will be sufficient.

NEEDLE: #22

YARNS: Separate the Persian yarn and use two threads; you will need the following amounts before separating:

1) palest yellow-white, 45 yds.
2) light gold, 10 yds.
3) dark gold, 15 yds.
4) pink, 8 yds.
5) bright orange, 6 yds.
6) dark red, 20 yds.
7) terracotta, 45 yds.
8) deep brown, 125 yds.
9) medium Delft blue, 20 yds.
10) light seafoam green, 12 yds.

STITCH: Basketweave

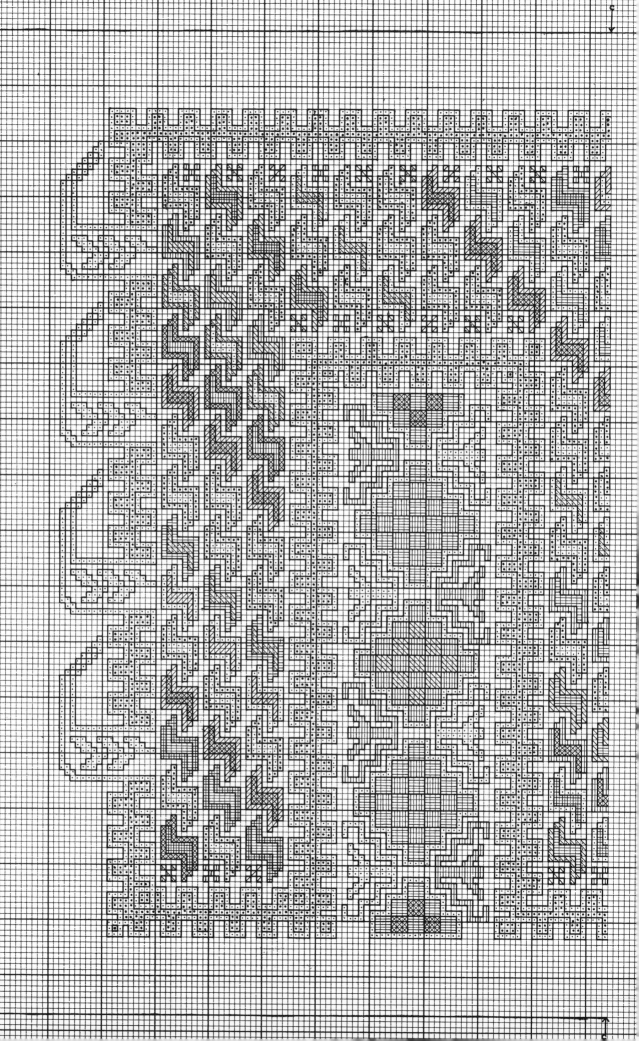

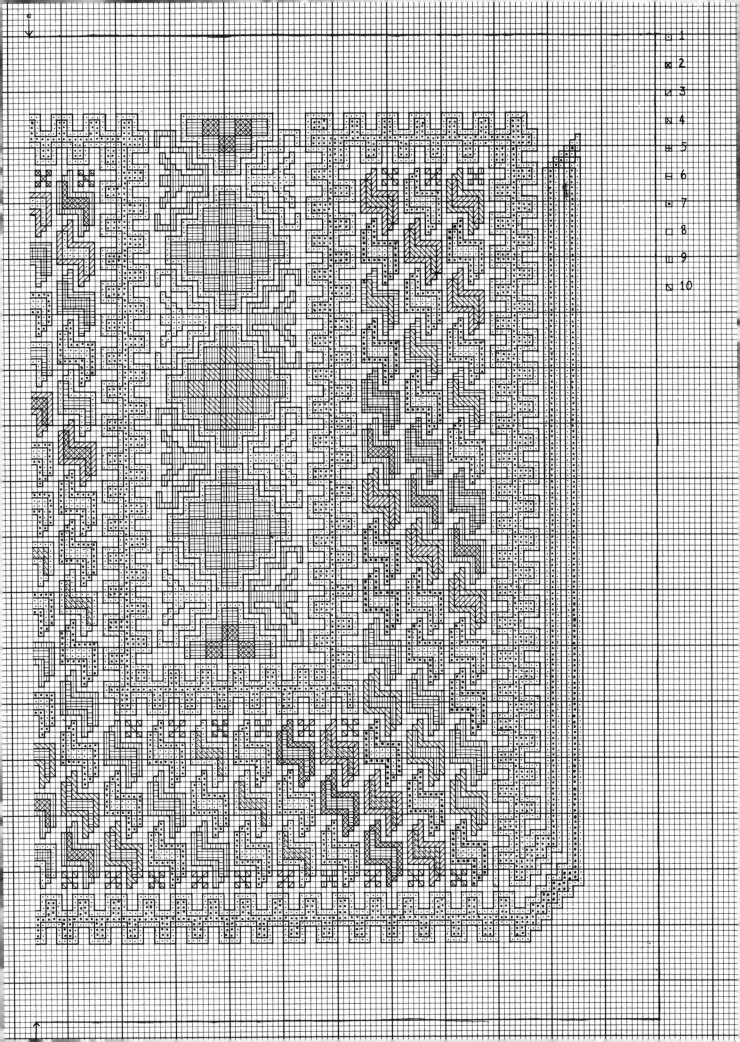

140

45. Kuba Cushion

19" × 16"

In the Caucasus Mountains, the town of Kuba gives its name to the type of carpet woven there, a fine example of which provides the central motif and coloring for this design.

CANVAS: 10 mesh to the inch. Design covers 189 mesh horizontally by 159 mesh vertically. A piece of canvas at least 21" by 18" will be sufficient.

NEEDLE: #18

YARNS: Use the full strand of Persian yarn in the following amounts:

1) white, 15 yds.
2) medium bright gold, 80 yds.
3) coral red, 130 yds.
4) medium gray, 55 yds.
5) deep Delft blue, 55 yds.

STITCH: Basketweave

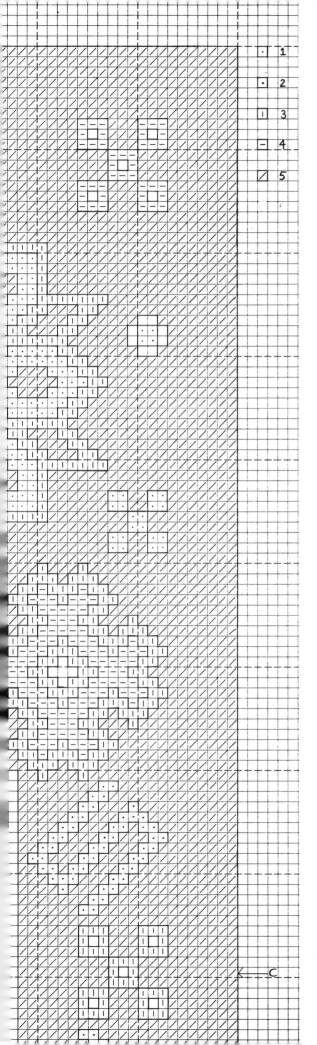

·	1
□	2
⊡	3
⊟	4
╱	5

K---C

46. Karabagh Cushion

18″ × 18″—Color Plate Page 129

The central motif of this design comes from a carpet of the Karabagh type, woven in the Azerbaijan Soviet Socialist Republic in the Caucasus Mountains.

CANVAS: 10 mesh to the inch. Design covers a 179-mesh square; a square of canvas at least 20″ by 20″ will be sufficient.

NEEDLE: #18

YARNS: Use the full strand of Persian yarn in the following amounts:

1) white, 20 yds.
2) medium bright gold, 35 yds.
3) coral red, 60 yds.
4) medium gray, 40 yds.
5) deep Delft blue, 160 yds.

STITCH: Basketweave

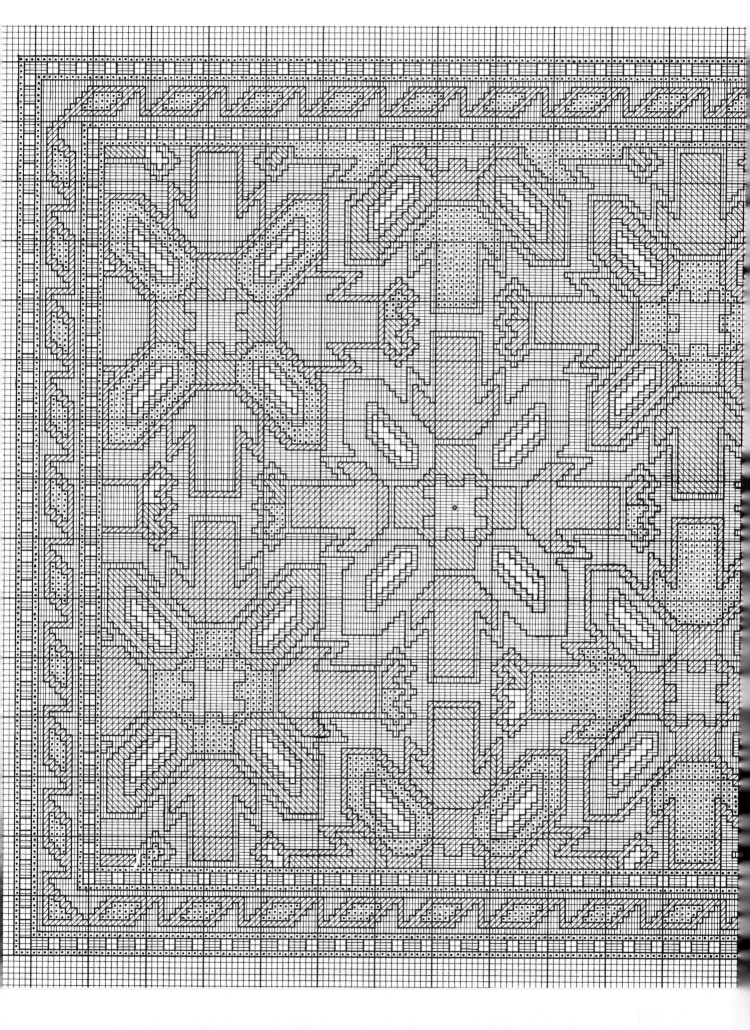

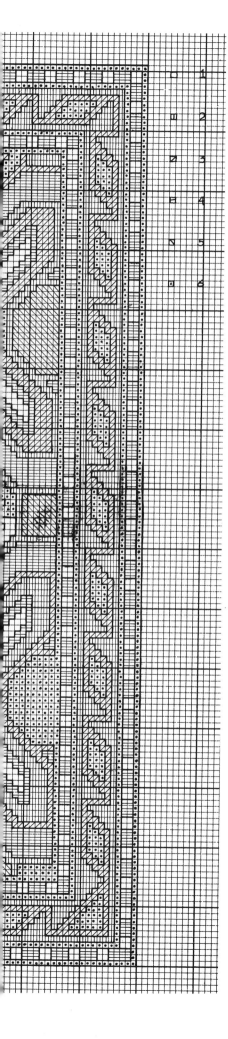

47. Shirvan Cushion

15" × 15"—Color Plate Page 129

Also from the Azerbaijan S. S. R. comes the original carpet motif used in this piece; the colors used are typical of those used in carpets of this Transcaucasian region near northern Iran.

CANVAS: 10 mesh to the inch. Design covers 153 mesh horizontally by 151 mesh vertically; a square of canvas at least 17 1/4" by 17 1/4" will be sufficient.

NEEDLE: #18

YARNS: Use the full strand of Persian yarn in the following amounts:

1) white, 20 yds.
2) lightest possible gold (beige), 50 yds.
3) bright medium gold, 45 yds.
4) dark red, 40 yds.
5) medium Delft blue, 25 yds.
6) dark Delft blue, 60 yds.

STITCH: Basketweave

48. Turkmenian Cushion

18 3/4″ × 15 3/4″—Color Plate Page 129

The border design of a carpet of the type known as Yomud, woven in the Soviet Socialist Republic of Turkmenia, inspired this design. The motif is described as a formalized bird, but I see it more as a moth or butterfly.

CANVAS: 10 mesh to the inch. Design covers 187 mesh horizontally by 157 mesh vertically; a piece of canvas at least 20 3/4″ by 17 3/4″ will be sufficient.

NEEDLE: #18
YARNS: Use the full strand of Persian yarn in the following amounts:
1) light yellow, 45 yds.
2) medium gold, 55 yds.
3) yellow-orange, 15 yds.
4) medium terracotta, 30 yds.
5) deep rust, 100 yds.
6) lilac, 35 yds.
7) deep brown, 35 yds.
8) black, 45 yds.
9) turquoise, 1 yd.
10) Kelly green, 1 yd.
11) jade green, 1 yd.
12) olive green, 1 yd.
STITCH: Basketweave

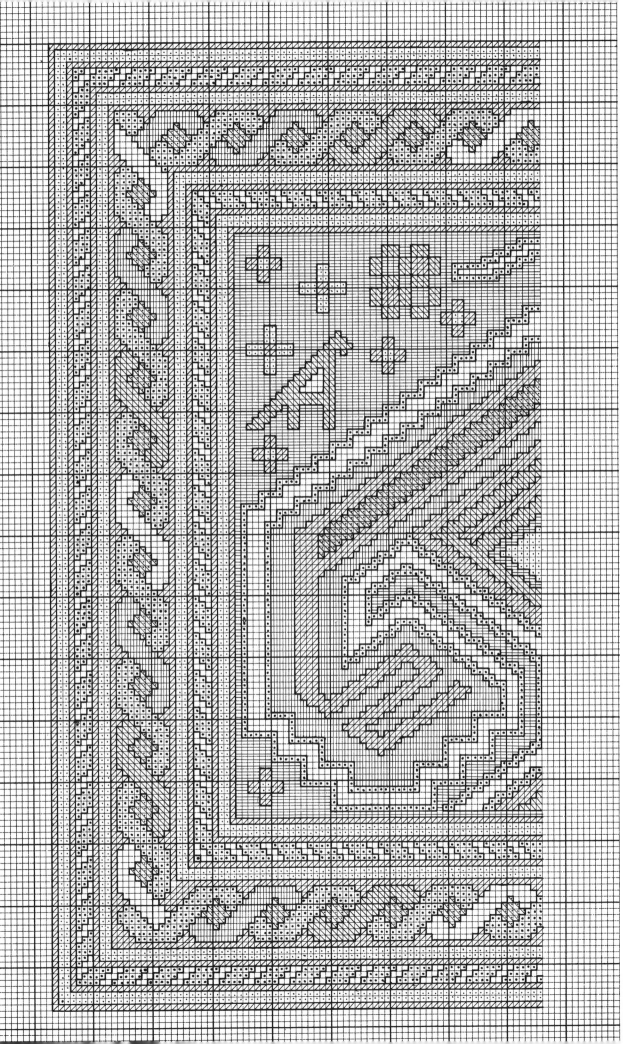

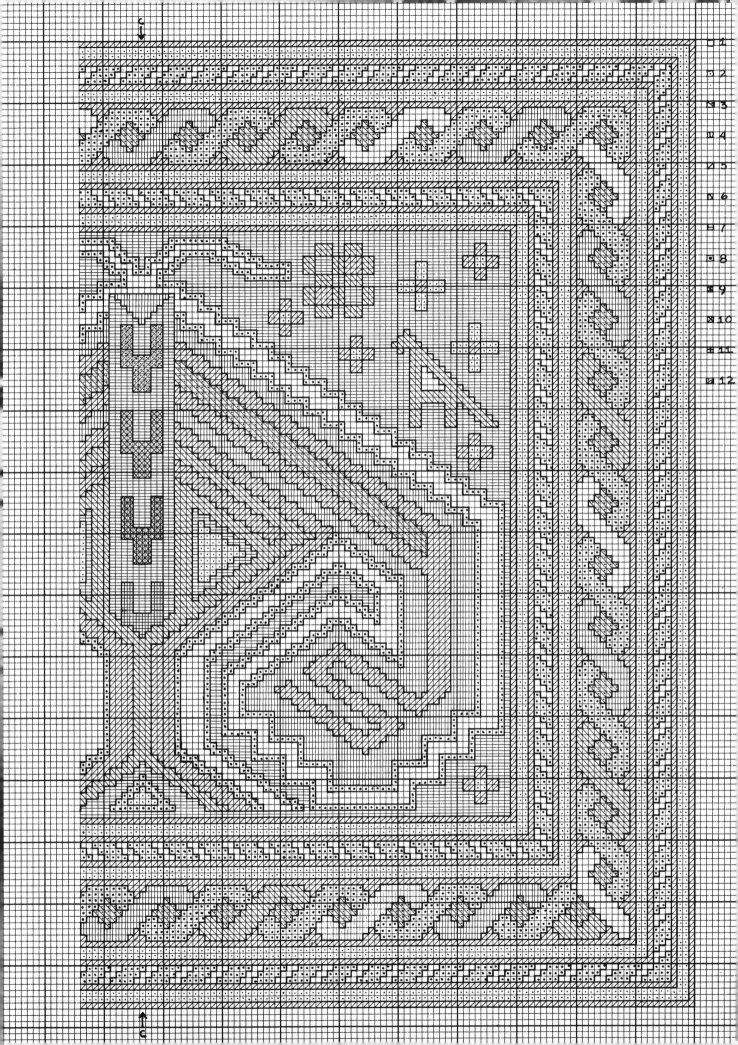

49. Turkmenian Design, Canvas Shoulder Bag

This design was worked on the canvas insert of the flap of a brown canvas shoulder bag made by Toni Totes of Vermont (see Sources). Following the graph for the preceding Turkmenian cushion, proceed as follows:

Center the moth motif along the vertical row of mesh in the center of the canvas insert. Have the base of the motif lie about two horizontal rows of mesh from the edge of the binding of the bag's flap. As with all canvas inserts of this type, you should lift the edge of the binding and work an extra mesh underneath, so that no uncovered canvas will show. The borders of the design will be eliminated and you may want to slightly rearrange the small motifs surrounding the moth. I stitched my initials plus a few of the small motifs in the extra area above the moth, and you might do the same. Choose a brown yarn for the background to match the shade of brown of the binding.

CANVAS: The canvas insert of the bag is 12 mesh to the inch.

NEEDLE: #20 or #22

YARNS: Separate the Persian yarn and use two threads; you will need the following amounts before separating:

1) light yellow, 12 yds.
2) medium gold, 4 yds.
3) yellow-orange, 4 yds.
4) medium terracotta, 16 yds.
5) deep rust, 15 yds.
6) lilac, 8 yds.
7) deep brown, 25 yds.
8) black, 15 yds.
9) turquoise, 1/2 yd.
10) Kelly green, 1/2 yd.
11) jade green, 1/2 yd.
12) olive green, 1/2 yd.

STITCH: Basketweave

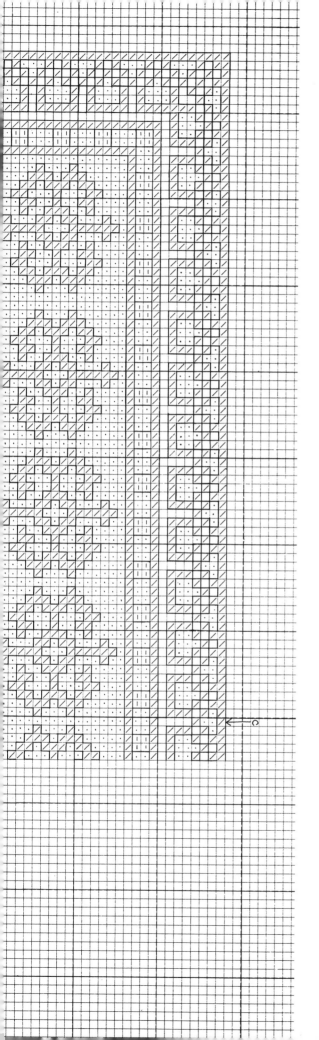

50. Baluchi Cushion

11" × 11"—Color Plate Page 136

The design for this piece comes from the central repeated motif of a carpet made by the Baluchis, a nomadic people of Iran. Its distinctive design and coloring are characteristic of the Turkoman type of carpet. You may prefer to use a brighter red than the coral I've used here.

CANVAS: 14 mesh to the inch. Design covers a 155-mesh square; a square of canvas at least 13" by 13" will be sufficient.

NEEDLE: #22

YARNS: Separate Persian yarn and use two threads; you will need the following amounts before separating:

1) white, 32 yds.
2) maize yellow, 14 yds.
3) coral red, 65 yds.
4) black, 50 yds.

STITCH: Basketweave

51. Byzantine Cushion

15 1/2″ × 15 1/2″—COLOR PLATE PAGE 131

The central motif and borders of this design were adapted from an Egyptian carpet of the Byzantine period (fourth–fifth centuries A.D.) in the collection of the Metropolitan Museum of Art. As the accompanying photograph illustrates, the design of the carpet is composed of several such motifs and borders, any of which could have been recombined to achieve a pleasing effect. The colors coincide as closely as possible with those of the original carpet.

CANVAS: 17 mesh to the inch. Design covers a 263-mesh square; a square of canvas at least 17 1/2″ by 17 1/2″ will be sufficient.

NEEDLE: #22

YARNS: Separate Persian yarn and use one thread; you will need the following amounts before separating:

1) white, 40 yds.
2) coral, 60 yds.
3) deep dusty rose or rosy rust, 30 yds.
4) light Delft blue, 20 yds.
5) medium Delft blue, 32 yds.
6) deep Delft blue, 4 yds.
7) medium taupe, 17 yds.

STITCH: Basketweave

NOTE: Following the graph will be quite simple; work the upper right quarter of the design, as given in the graph. Then turn the graph clockwise 90 degrees. Work the lower left quarter of the design *without* repeating the center row of small grid squares on the graph, which will run across the top when the graph is turned this way. But *do* repeat the *vertical* row of small grid squares which will run along the left edge of the graph. Turn the graph clockwise 90 degrees twice again to work the other two quarters in the same fashion, repeating and not repeating the center rows of small grid squares where appropriate; this will be obvious, especially where the border diamonds continue from one quarter to the next.

52. Coptic Cushion

19 1/4″ × 15″

An Egyptian textile, woven in the first centuries of the Christian era, provides the design for this piece. The original indigo blue of the textile seems to have aged to a deep brownish violet, but I chose to use a deep burgundy for this design, as the present color of the textile would be nearly impossible to replicate. However, almost any deep tone would be handsome for the design.

CANVAS: 13 mesh to the inch. Design covers 245 mesh horizontally by 195 mesh vertically; a piece of canvas at least 21 1/4″ by 17″ will be sufficient.

NEEDLE: #22

YARNS: Separate Persian yarn and use two threads; you will need the following amounts before separating:

1) white, 60 yds.
2) deep burgundy, 160 yds.

STITCH: Basketweave

NOTE: Watch for the asterisks on the graph, which indicate where the number of stitches on either side of the "stem" in the border motif changes from three to two; remember to repeat this when working the other three quarters of the design.

155

Asian Designs

53. Assam Design I, Wall Hanging

16 1/4″ × 14 1/2″—COLOR PLATES PAGES 132, 133

This and the following design are both derived from the same original textile from the Garo region of Assam, India, in the collection of the Peabody Museum. The textile is a long, relatively narrow woven strip; the design consists of many bands. The bands repeat similar diamond motifs, with what seem to me several distinct color harmonies in operation. I found it impractical to try to contain these shifts in harmony within a reasonable area; so I decided to develop two separate designs, each with its own harmony, but with similar treatment of the red ground continuing throughout each design. This is the first.

CANVAS: 14 mesh to the inch. Design covers 227 mesh horizontally by 203 mesh vertically; a piece of canvas at least 18 1/4″ by 16 1/2″ will be sufficient.

NEEDLE: #22

YARNS: Separate Persian yarn and use two threads; you will need the following amounts before separating:
1) lemon yellow, 40 yds.
2) lime green, 45 yds.
3) bright red, 120 yds.
4) medium violet, 5 yds.
5) deep bright blue, 35 yds.
6) black, 7 yds.

STITCH: Basketweave

54. Assam Design II, Wall Hanging

17″ × 16 1/2″—COLOR PLATE PAGE 132

See preceding design for notes on the derivation of this piece.

CANVAS: 17 mesh to the inch. Design covers 289 mesh horizontally by 277 mesh vertically; a piece of canvas at least 19″ by 18 1/2″ will be sufficient.

NEEDLE: #22

YARNS: Separate Persian yarn and use one thread; you will need the following amounts before separating:

1) white, 15 yds.
2) light hot pink, 30 yds
3) bright red, 95 yds.
4) black, 15 yds.

STITCH: Basketweave

NOTE: Repeat entire area given in the graph, but reversing it, as in a mirror image, three more times to the left, ending with an extra vertical row of pattern to correspond with the first such row at right edge. This will give you the entire upper half of the design. For the lower half, repeat everything above the horizontal center mesh, as marked on the graph, in mirror image again.

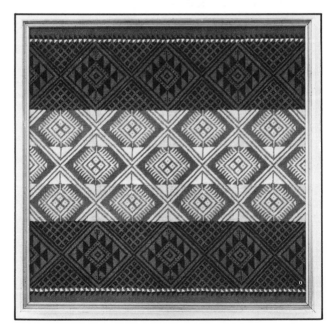

55. Kashmir Cushion

16″ × 15″—COLOR PLATE PAGE 95

An exquisite silk and gold-thread textile in the collection of the Peabody Museum, from the Indian state of Kashmir, inspired this design.

CANVAS: 14 mesh to the inch. Design covers 225 mesh horizontally by 209 mesh vertically; a piece of canvas at least 18″ by 17″ will be sufficient.

NEEDLE: #20

YARNS: Separate Persian yarn and use two threads; you will need the following amount before separating:

2) deep dusty rose, 200 yds.

Bucilla Spotlight, using a single strand:

1) gold, 1 1/2 spools

STITCH: Basketweave. You may use Scotch stitch in the small squares in the border which cover three mesh by three mesh.

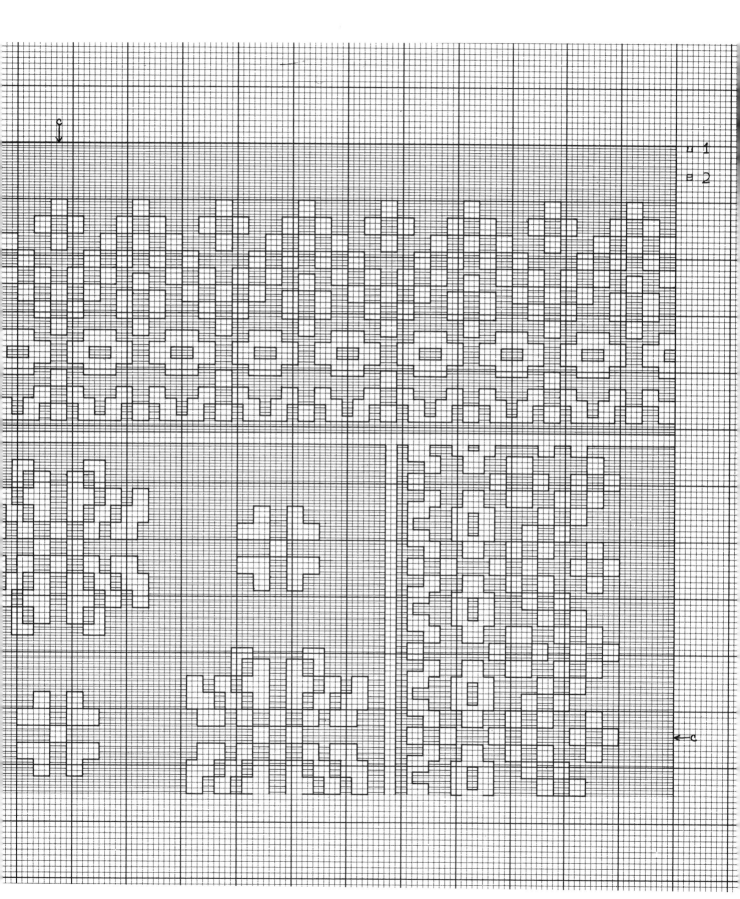

56. Punjab Cushion

17" × 15 1/2"—COLOR PLATE PAGE 96

A woman's blanket cape from the western Pahari-Kanawri tribe of Punjab, in northern India, provides the bold design and unusual coloring of this piece. The original textile is in the collection of the Peabody Museum.

CANVAS: 10 mesh to the inch. Design covers 168 mesh horizontally by 156 mesh vertically; a piece of canvas at least 19" by 17 1/2" will be sufficient.

NEEDLE: #18

YARNS: Use the full strand of Persian yarn in the following amounts:
1) white, 34 yds.
2) lemon yellow, 40 yds.
3) bright red, 40 yds.
4) lilac, 18 yds.
5) deep bright blue, 12 yds.
6) black, or deepest brown, 80 yds.

STITCH: Basketweave

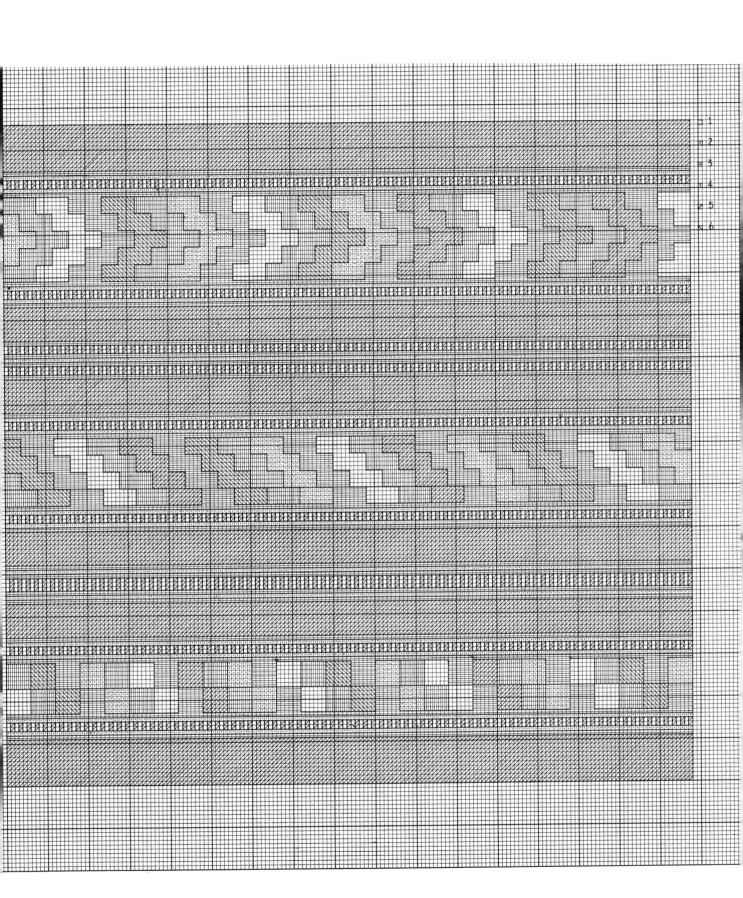

57. Burmese Cushion

16 1/4″ × 14 3/4″—COLOR PLATE PAGE 90

A woman's skirt from the Kachin people of Burma, in the collection of the Peabody Museum, provides the pattern bands for this piece, and its unusual coloring.

CANVAS: 14 mesh to the inch. Design covers 227 mesh horizontally by 205 mesh vertically; a piece of canvas at least 18 1/4″ by 16 3/4″ will be sufficient.

NEEDLE: #22

YARNS: Separate Persian yarn and use two threads; you will need the following amounts before separating:

1) coral, 80 yds.
2) dark red, 80 yds.
3) light hot pink, 10 yds.
4) yellow-orange, 22 yds.
5) turquoise, 25 yds.
6) black, 120 yds.

STITCH: Basketweave

NOTE: The pattern for each band repeats in the sequences given, past the vertical center to the left edge. However, the colors of the motifs change from right to left as follows:

Band A: swastika motifs: yellow, pink, turquoise, yellow, pink.

Band B: inner diamond: turquoise, yellow, pink.

Band C: chevrons: red, turquoise, coral, yellow, coral, red, coral, turquoise, red, coral, yellow, coral, red, turquoise, coral (last chevron is fragmented).

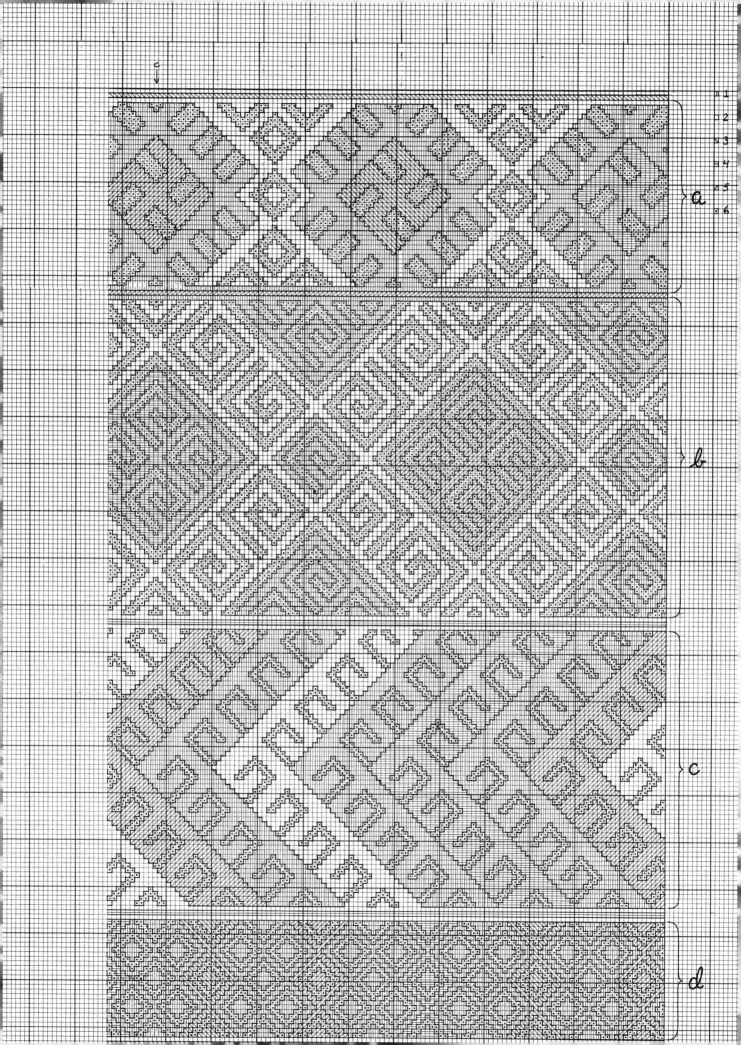

58. Burmese Design, Mini Purse

COLOR PLATE PAGE 90

This little purse, with a 10-mesh-to-the-inch canvas insert sewn into the flap, comes from Needlepoint, U.S.A. (see SOURCES). Find the center mesh of the canvas insert, then find an interesting area of Band C on the graph for the preceding Burmese cushion and, following the graph, start at a point along the horizontal center of the band. This particular sequence of the pattern requires using the full strand of Persian yarn, with a #18 needle, in the following amounts:

1) coral, 17 yds.
2) dark red, 5 yds.
4) yellow-orange, 8 yds.
5) turquoise, 6 yds.

59. Moro Cushion

14" × 13 1/2"—COLOR PLATE PAGE 134

The pattern and unusual coloring of this design come from a textile, woven by the Moro people of the Philippines, now in the collection of the Peabody Museum.

CANVAS: 13 mesh to the inch. Design spans 179 mesh horizontally by 174 mesh vertically. A piece of canvas at least 16" by 15 1/2" will be sufficient.

NEEDLE: #20 or #22

YARNS: Separate Persian yarn and use two threads; you will need the following amounts before separating:

1) white, 14 yds.
2) lemon yellow, 16 yds.
3) hot pink, 13 yds.
4) yellow-orange, 16 yds.
5) turquoise, 22 yds.
6) magenta, 19 yds.
7) medium rust, 70 yds.

STITCH: Knitting

NOTE: The small grid squares of the graph represent the *mesh* of canvas *covered* by the Knitting stitches. (See page 19, under FOLLOWING THE GRAPHS, and refer to the stitch diagram on page 28.) Repeat entire bracketed area; end with border along lower edge.

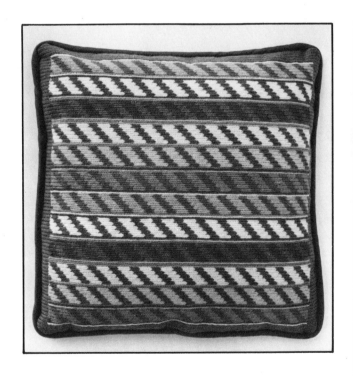

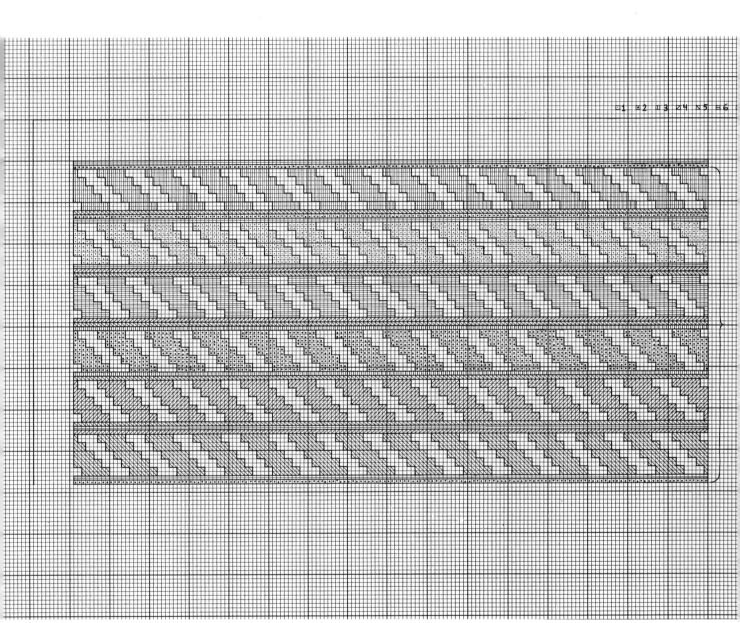

60. Moro Design, Luggage Straps

COLOR PLATE PAGE 134

CANVAS: To make three luggage straps, each approximately 2" by 16 1/4", you need a piece of 13-mesh-to-the-inch canvas at least 10 1/2" by 18". This will give you about an inch between straps and all around (see photo).

NEEDLE: #20 or #22

YARNS: Separate Persian yarn and use two threads; you will need the following amounts before separating:

1) white, 8 yds.
2) lemon yellow, 14 yds.
3) hot pink, 13 yds.
4) yellow-orange, 16 yds.
5) turquoise, 20 yds.
6) magenta, 20 yds.
7) medium rust, 40 yds.

STITCH: Knitting

NOTE: Work five rows of Knitting stitch in rust, each row covering 28 canvas mesh, across top of area to be covered for first strap. Then follow the graph for the preceding Moro cushion bands, repeating the entire sequence of bands twice, as you would to work the cushion, then repeating this sequence only as far as four more bands, to make 16 bands in all. End with two or three of the fine stripes and the five rows of rust, as at the top of strap. Follow the same procedure for the other two straps.

The straps may then be lightly steam pressed, cut out, and then backed with a compatible fabric, leaving ends open with a half inch extra of backing fabric. Attach to stand (ours is from Sudberry House; see SOURCES) with a heavy-duty staple gun.

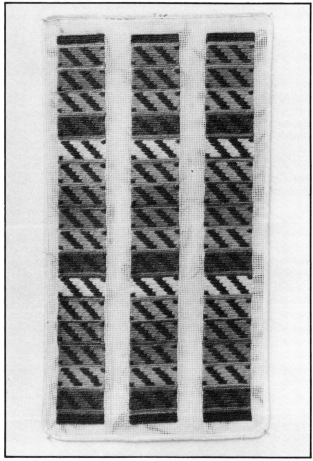

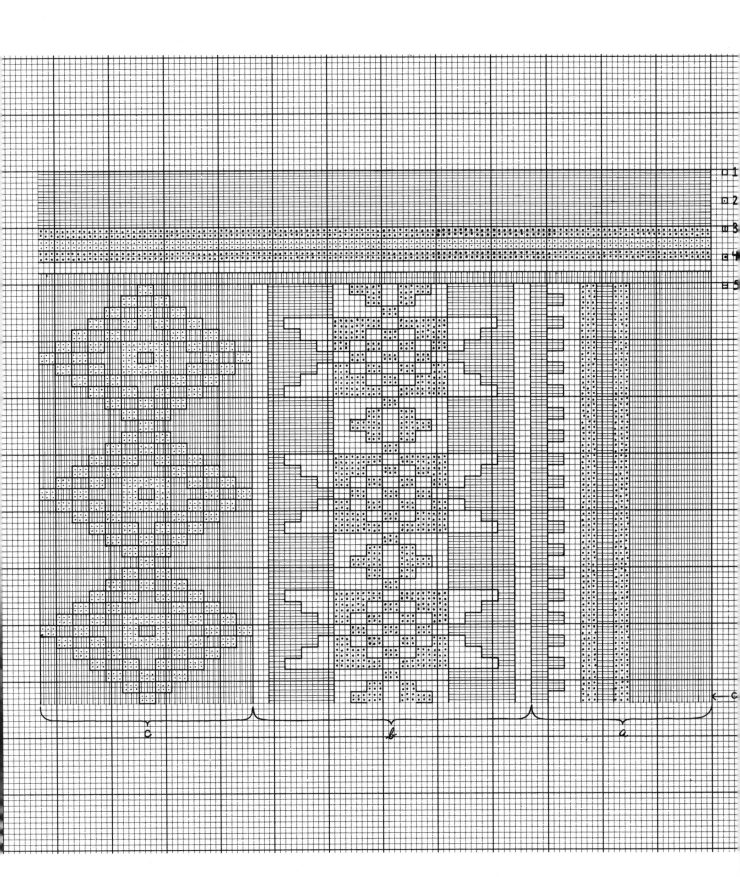

61. Indonesian Design, Piano-Bench Cover

38 3/4″ × 18 1/2″—COLOR PLATE PAGE 95

Another fine textile, in the collection of the Peabody Museum, inspired this design.

CANVAS: 10 mesh to the inch. Design covers 387 mesh horizontally by 186 mesh vertically; a piece of canvas at least 41″ by 21″ will be sufficient.

NEEDLE: #18

YARNS: Use the full strand of Persian yarn in the following amounts:

1) ivory, 110 yds.
2) light gold, 30 yds.
3) medium taupe, 100 yds.
4) medium terracotta (rust), 80 yds.
5) deep rust brown, 160 yds.

STITCH: Cashmere, alternating

NOTE: Work design area given in the graph, then, continuing to the left, repeat section "b" three more times and section "c" twice more, alternating. End with border "a." This will give you the upper half of the design; you will then continue down from the horizontal center mark, repeating the entire design from that point in mirror image.

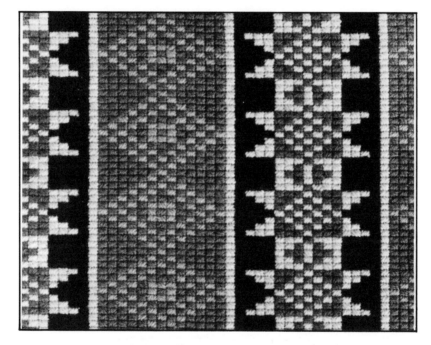

62. Siamese Design, Canvas Tote

15″ × 13 1/2″—Color Plate Page 89

The design and coloring of this piece derive from an extraordinary textile from Thailand in the collection of the Peabody Museum. Originally woven for a skirt, the fabric is an outstanding example of a style typical of the area once known as West Lao. There seems to have been much competition among the women weavers to achieve the most beautiful designs of this type.

CANVAS: 17 mesh to the inch. Design covers 257 mesh horizontally by 225 mesh vertically; a piece of canvas at least 17″ by 15 1/2″ will be sufficient.

NEEDLE: #22

YARNS: Separate Persian yarn and use one thread; you will need the following amounts before separating:

1) lemon yellow, 65 yds.
2) lime green, 22 yds.
3) bright orange, 20 yds.
4) bright red, 40 yds.
5) black, 60 yds.

STITCH: Basketweave

Note: This design was expertly mounted into a large canvas tote by Elizabeth Birchfield of Accessories Unlimited (see Sources).

172

63. Japanese Tasuki Cushion

16" × 16"—Color Plate Page 95

The motif for this piece comes from a Japanese garment textile, woven in a *tasuki* pattern consisting of straight lines intersecting on the diagonal to form a diamond-shaped lattice. Birds fitted into the *tasuki* lattice produce this particular variation called the "bird *tasuki*." *Tasuki* is one of a number of patterns referred to as "*yūsoku* patterns," textile designs of Chinese origin developed during the Heian period for use on ceremonial garments. The Heian period (A.D. 794–1185) is characterized by a movement toward "Japanization" of cultural ideas and institutions introduced under previous Chinese influence. These motifs became thoroughly established in Japanese usage and gradually took on characteristics of Japanese taste, finally losing all marked differences from other native decorative patterns. They are the source of ground patterns on Nō theatrical costumes, and the shape of the costumes also derives from the shape of the traditional *yūsoku* garment.

CANVAS: 14 mesh to the inch. Design covers a 223-mesh square; a square of canvas at least 18" by 18" will be sufficient.

NEEDLE: #20

YARNS: Separate Persian yarn and use two threads; you will need the following amount before separating:

1) medium Delft blue, 130 yds.

Bucilla Spotlight, using a single strand:

2) gold, 1 1/2 spools

STITCH: Basketweave

Sources

Accessories Unlimited, Main Street, Cornish, Maine 04020. Write to Elizabeth Birchfield for catalog of made-to-order canvas bags. Your needlepoint piece can be mounted into the construction of any of the bags shown, and you may choose a canvas color to coordinate with your piece.

Bucilla Yarns, 30-20 Thomson Avenue, Long Island City, N.Y. 11101. Bucilla yarns are available in yarn shops and department stores across the country. Write to Bucilla to find out which stores in your area carry them.

Miracles with the Binding Stitch, by Joan Young. To purchase this booklet, write to Joan Young, 1518 Spruce Drive, Kalamazoo, Michigan 49008.

Needlepoint, U.S.A., 37 West 57th Street, New York, New York 10019. Many prefinished items with canvas inserts or openings for mounting your needlework, made by Needlepoint, U.S.A., may be purchased in yarn shops across the country or you may write them for their brochure and retail price list.

Nēpo Needlework Markers, Sanford Corporation, Box 60104, Bellwood, Illinois 60104. These markers are available in yarn shops across the country. Write for the name of the dealer in your area.

Alice Peterson Company, 207 East Franklin Avenue, El Segundo, California 90245. These fully fabricated items with canvas inserts for needlepoint are available in yarn shops across the country. Write to Alice Peterson Company to find out which shops in your area carry their line.

Sudberry House, Box 421, Old Lyme, Connecticut 06371. These fine wood products for mounting needlework are available in yarn shops throughout the country. Or write to Sudberry House for their retail color catalog at $2.00.

Joan Toggitt, Ltd., 246 Fifth Avenue, New York, New York 10001. Write to them for the name of the shop in your area that carries their perfectly square, "orange-lined" canvas.

Toni Totes of Vermont, Inc., Route 100, South Londonderry, Vermont 05155. These prefinished canvas totes, etc., with canvas inserts may be purchased at many local yarn shops, or write for their mail-order catalog.

Bibliography

BIRRELL, VERLA, *The Textile Arts*, Schocken Books, New York, 1974.

DAVISON, MARGUERITE PORTER, *A Handweaver's Pattern Book*, Marguerite Porter Davison, publisher, Swarthmore, Pa., 1971.

GANS-RUEDIN, E., *The Connoisseur's Guide to Oriental Carpets*, Charles E. Tuttle Company, Rutland, Vt. and Tokyo, 1971.

GRIMBLE, IAN, *Scottish Clans and Tartans*, Tudor Publishing Company, New York, 1973.

KAHLENBERG, MARY HUNT and BERLANT, ANTHONY, *The Navajo Blanket*, catalog of the exhibition, Praeger Publishers, Inc., in association with the Los Angeles County Museum of Art, 1972.

KENT, KATE P., *Introducing West African Cloth*, published in conjunction with an exhibition of African textiles, Denver Museum of Natural History, 1971.

LAMB, VENICE AND ALISTAIR, *The Lamb Collection of West African Weaving*, catalog of the exhibition, the Textile Museum, Washington, D.C., 1975.

LIEBETRAU, PREBEN, *Oriental Rugs in Color*, The Macmillan Company, New York, 1972.

LUBELL, CECIL, editor, *Textile Collections of the World*, Volumes 1, 2 and 3, Van Nostrand Reinhold Company, New York, 1976, 1977.

MIZOGUCHI, SABURO, *Arts of Japan I, Design Motifs*, John Weatherhill, Inc., New York, and Shibundō, Tokyo, 1973.

SIEBER, ROY, *African Textiles and Decorative Arts*, catalog of the exhibition, Museum of Modern Art, New York, 1972.

My Special Thanks...

for so beautifully executing the designs:

Mary E. Adams, Brunswick, Maine
Mary Aquila, Bayside, New York
Miriam W. Barndt-Webb, Brunswick, Maine
Desneige Bernier, Pejepscot, Maine
Maryellen Coles, Cape Elizabeth, Maine
Marilyn Habel Dwyer, Brunswick, Maine
Pamela B. Galvin, Brunswick, Maine
Ann Ward Goffin, Brunswick, Maine
Stella Grottalio, Bayside, New York
Pamela T. Hatch, New York, New York
Cara J. Hayes, Brunswick, Maine
Jane Hazelton, Topsham, Maine
Margaret D. Higgins, Brunswick, Maine
Jaci Holmes, Brunswick, Maine
Nancy L. Johansen, Brunswick, Maine
Bella Kasowitz, West Haven, Connecticut
Hsin-i Langlois, Brunswick, Maine
Judith A. Leaman, Brunswick, Maine
Marcy McGuire, Brunswick, Maine
Helen L. McKay, Battle Creek, Michigan
Chris Millar, Brunswick, Maine
Abby Neal, Brunswick, Maine
Maureen Thomas Osier, Topsham, Maine
Elizabeth Plissonneau, Pompano Beach, Florida
Madeleine Plissonneau, Paris
Marguerite Rafter, Wiscasset, Maine
Marion H. Redlon, Bath, Maine
Marie E. Rieser, Wickford, Rhode Island
Margaret T. Ring, Brunswick, Maine
Pat Robinson, Brunswick, Maine
Elena M. S. Silander, Brunswick, Maine
Vita Simone, Flushing, New York, my sister-in-law
Betty S. Smith, South Harpswell, Maine
Ebba F. Sonne, Morton Grove, Illinois
Carol Stark, Brunswick, Maine

Gloria Steinbrenner, Battle Creek, Michigan
Judith A. Thornton, Brunswick, Maine
Mary Hoffman Treworgy, Brunswick, Maine
Diane Kavookjian Young, Darien, Connecticut

for finishing the cushions, etc., so handsomely:

Rosalie Pinette, Parkview Cleaners, Brunswick, Maine
Marion Soper, Ye Yarn Barn, Brunswick, Maine
Gloria Stuart, Yankee Yarns, Brunswick, Maine
Sally Tenner, The Village Yarn Shop, New Haven, Connecticut

for such fine upholstering:

G. Pelletier, Lisbon Falls, Maine
The Schultz Company, Falmouth, Maine

for such prompt and expert framing:

Curtis Framing, Brunswick, Maine

for generously giving of their time to proof the graphs:

Maryann Crockett, Pam Galvin, Dian Jordan, Hilda Overman, Eve
Rittmeyer, Elena Silander, and Joan Wood, all of Brunswick.